PSYCHEDELIC
— MARINE —

A Transformational Journey
from Afghanistan to the Amazon

ALEX SEYMOUR

Park Street Press
Rochester, Vermont • Toronto, Canada

Park Street Press
One Park Street
Rochester, Vermont 05767
www.ParkStPress.com

Park Street Press is a division of Inner Traditions International

Library of Congress Cataloging-in-Publication Data
Names: Seymour, Alex, author.
Title: Psychedelic Marine : a transformational journey from Afghanistan to the
    Amazon / Alex Seymour.
Other titles: Transformational journey from Afghanistan to the Amazon
Description: Rochester, Vermont : Park Street Press, [2016]
Identifiers: LCCN 2016003883 (print) | LCCN 2016004794 (e-book) |
    ISBN 9781620555798 (pbk.) | ISBN 9781620555804 (e-book)
Subjects: LCSH: Seymour, Alex. | Afghan War, 2001—Personal narratives,
    British. | Great Britain. Royal Marines. Commando, 42—Biography. | Afghan
    War, 2001—Campaigns—Afghanistan—Helmand. | Marines—Great Britain—
    Biography. | Veterans—Drug use—Great Britain. | Ayahuasca Ceremony—
    Peru. | Ayahuasca—Psychotropic effects. | Hallucinogenic drugs and religious
    experience—Peru.
Classification: LCC DS371.413 .S47 2016 (print) | LCC DS371.413 (e-book) |
    DDC 958.104/742092—dc23
LC record available at http://lccn.loc.gov/2016003883

Printed and bound in the United States by P. A. Hutchison Company

10 9 8 7 6 5 4 3 2 1

Text design and layout by Priscilla Baker
This book was typeset in Garamond Premier Pro with Intro used as a display
typeface

The images in the goggles and on the spine of the cover are by Pablo Amaringo
from *The Ayahuasca Visions of Pablo Amaringo*

To send correspondence to the author of this book, mail a first-class letter to
the author c/o Inner Traditions • Bear & Company, One Park Street, Rochester,
VT 05767, and we will forward the communication.

PSYCHEDELIC
— MARINE —

"Alex Seymour deployed to Afghanistan to test himself and rediscover his full potential through warfare. Little did he know it was a stepping stone to his hardest test as a warrior—taking ayahuasca in the jungle in Peru where he would surrender to his greatest fears and find that the ultimate answers had been inside himself all along."

IAN BENOUIS, WEST POINT GRADUATE,
FORMER BLACK HAWK HELICOPTER PILOT AND
COMBAT VETERAN, AND CANNABIS ACTIVIST

"A revealing juxtaposition of two life experiences most can only begin to imagine, bringing to life the stress and fatigue of a marine's lot in Afghanistan and his subsequent metaphysical quest for enlightenment."

JAKE WOOD, AUTHOR OF *AMONG YOU:
THE EXTRAORDINARY TRUE STORY OF A SOLDIER BROKEN BY WAR*

"More than a report of one marine's experience, this book is a call to the armed forces medical corps, the Veterans Administration, and veterans' groups . . . to fund research to support treating PTSD with ayahuasca and other psychedelics."

THOMAS B. ROBERTS, PH.D.,
AUTHOR OF *THE PSYCHEDELIC FUTURE OF THE MIND*

"A true story of a man who pushed the boundaries way beyond any semblance of comfort zone through the devastation and horror of war and who went on to find healing, transformation, and salvation by dissolving the boundaries of ordinary consciousness into the vast spaces of the transpersonal realm."

TOM SOLOWAY PINKSON, PH.D., VISION QUEST LEADER, PSYCHOLOGIST,
AND AUTHOR OF *THE SHAMANIC WISDOM OF THE HUICHOL*

"*Psychedelic Marine* is a unique, mind-stretching, powerful story that captivates you from page one to the end. If you want your spirit to be lifted and inspired and to know what is possible beyond the boundaries of convention, this is a must-read."

CHRIS WALTON, MSc, BEST-SELLING AUTHOR OF *THE GAMMA MINDSET*

For my wife, Julia, and for JJ Chalmers

Entheogen: a consciousness-altering substance, usually natural, such as a plant or mushroom that is used in a sacred context to explore the self and facilitate healing. Literally it means "generating the divine within." The etymology is Greek: *entheos,* which means "full of god, inspired or possessed," and *genesthai,* to "come into being." Thus, an entheogen is a psychotropic substance that causes one to become inspired or to experience feelings of inspiration, especially in a spiritual or revelatory manner.

Wikipedia

Contents

PART 2

— THE MYTHIC VOYAGE —

Prologue

It was masochism. Why else would anyone put himself through those extremities again? I was twenty years older, supposedly wiser. Back at HQ in the UK nine months earlier, the marine company commander had ventured: "If you want to get back in the field so badly, be careful what you wish for. You might find yourself in Helmand as point man, point section. You know our blokes are getting blown to bits out there, right?"

Roger that. I was now, literally, back in the field in a godforsaken corner of Helmand, Afghanistan. Men from my commando unit had already been killed, and here I was, the wretched point man at the head of an advancing arrowhead patrol formation, an offensive tactical formation that had remained unchanged in hundreds of years. I watched every step through the field, as we had no cover for three hundred meters in every direction. Gunshots from firefights rang out to the left and right of us. As dusk transitioned to night, illumination mortar shells burst like fireworks in the sky, lighting up the marines on either side of me in a flickering, eerie glow. We had broken cover from a tree line, and the only way to our objective was to patrol through this wide open field. Dead ahead was another tree line, behind which were several Afghan mud compounds. It was only a matter of time before the enemy opened fire from their perfect vantage point, aiming to commit murder. All nine of the men in my section were in an optimal kill zone. I had never felt more exposed, despite the protection, and crushing weight, of my body armor and kit. I knew that for the enemy, *now* was the time. For the hundredth time I wondered if my body armor chest plate would stop a bullet from entering my torso. I hoped the photo taped inside my helmet of my kids sitting in a wood full of bluebells would prove to be an effective talisman. Time would tell . . .

Be careful what you wish for . . . I had volunteered for this, and the fact that my wish had come true was either some kind of cosmic joke or proof that my strong intentions really had manifested into reality. We had been patrolling for six brutal, hot hours. The sweat running into my eyes had stopped stinging, as my eyes had grown used to it. The green bandanna beneath my helmet was saturated and useless at absorbing sweat.

Instinct urged us to break and run for the cover of the tree line ahead, but that kind of lapse in discipline would put us in more danger because there would be no chance to scan the ground for buried IEDs (improvised explosive devices). We crept forward slowly as trained. I wanted a second set of eyes—one to scan the ground constantly for IEDs and another to peer into the black "murder holes" punched into crumbling compound walls—those perfect lairs for enemy snipers. We trudged forward, now only forty meters from the safety of the tree line. The distance dwindled to twenty meters, then ten. Finally, we sank gasping for breath into an irrigation ditch, which afforded us some cover. One hundred patrols nailed, I thought, and another hundred to go. Just as crawling forward on your guts when checking out a suspected IED is a nerve shredder, so is the role of point man.

When I wasn't totally focused on staying alive in that field and now in the ditch, random thoughts slipped through my mind. Were my twenty years of corporate life after my first stint in the marines really so vacuous that I had been driven out here to feel something intense, to derive some higher value and meaning from life? Or was I a masochist? Ultimately, I would end those pointless thoughts with a resounding, Who cares? I was here now—deal with it. With half a tour left to crack, the only way to squeeze any vestige of morale out of myself was to conjure up a new mission, something to sustain me when, or if, I lived through this and exited this hellhole. I had no idea at that time, while taking cover in that ditch, that an undertaking equally as extreme as the Helmand front line loomed. I didn't know that a wild and enlightening adventure awaited me in the darkest parts of the Amazon jungle, hundreds of miles from civilization with a shaman and his troupe of loyal Natives and that my war-addled mind would be purified by powerful hallucinogenic potions. I didn't know that I would find myself adrift downriver on a mythic voyage of discovery led by a colossus of a man who appeared to be going insane . . .

But right then, in that muddy ditch, surrounded by exhausted marines, with the crackle of radio chatter in one ear and the staccato of gunfire in the other, I vowed that if I made it out of here in one piece, I was going in deep—deep into mystery and headlong into regenesis.

PART 1

THE SECRET THAT CAN'T BE TOLD

1

99.99% Need Not Apply

In 2009 I was in my early forties, married with two children, and with a successful career in the IT industry. I abandoned it all to become a Taliban hunter.

If forced to identify a single motivation for reentering the marines after a twenty-year absence and seeking a one-year tour in Afghanistan, I would have to admit it was the desire to escape metropolitan life and all its constraints. But it was more complex than that. I also felt the need to be tested and to do some good rather than to be merely transacting deals and striving for some measure of corporate "success." Instead of contributing I just consumed. With mounting introspection I realized success felt increasingly hollow, devoid of any true value. I worked in business development for a global multibillion dollar technology firm headquartered in Silicon Valley, California. I was on the cusp of ten years of employment and dumb enough to be proud of it. I knew that all businesses and governments wanted the same thing—information superiority, agility, speed, security, mobility—and we delivered it all: power and competitive advantage . . . for a price. My standard of living was good. But while my career could be satisfying, the working conditions had become intolerable thanks to a toxic, sociopathic boss—otherwise known as a prick. A walking buzz kill. My colleagues thought it inevitable that he would be let go soon enough. I considered how I could bide my time until that happened. It crossed my mind that a trip to Afghanistan in a commando unit could be the golden ticket out of that life.

My greatest fear had always been a lifetime of stupefying mediocrity. Compared to corporate life Afghanistan represented adventure. Life had become a homogenized celebration of mildness, all hint of wild ventures shooed away like moths in a wardrobe. Irrespective of the political intent of the war, history was being made, excitement guaranteed, and I had had it once—twenty years before when I had joined the marines as an innocent straight from school. Now, once again, for some twisted reason, I craved physical hardship, pushing limits, being tested until something broke.

Maybe my childhood was to blame. Isn't that what is supposed to be at the root of all complexes? By the time I was twelve, my mother was twice divorced and father number three was in the hot seat. My biological father had left when I was two. My first stepfather had been violent, inflicting beatings on my brothers and me on an almost daily basis. He wasn't evil, just damaged by the echo of his own father's horrors during the Second World War. Bedtime until the age of twelve was 6 p.m. on the nose, which happened to be when he arrived home. The verbal and physical abuse had an adverse effect on my self-esteem, and my little brothers' confidence fared no better. It was many years before I realized that he had inadvertently given me the ability to channel aggression—a trait that would have value in my future career. My mother left him when I was twelve.

From the ages of six to eleven, despite a less than rosy home life, life outside the house was good. Home was in a village on the outskirts of Bristol. Half a mile from our house was a huge hill called Dundry. As children we would walk a mile or so to the top, where there was an Iron Age fort, and be mesmerized by the view. The hill was a thousand feet high, and you could see for fifteen miles in every direction. The north afforded a view of Bristol—magnificent—and even at nine years old it was easy to admire the creativity and industrious effort it took to build such a modern city. In contrast, facing south, there was nothing but open, rolling English countryside where the counties of Avon and Somerset panned out in all their rustic glory. Meadows, lakes, and woods provided a beautiful vista out to the horizon. My friends and I would also ride our bikes for miles and miles into what we considered to be the wilderness for the exhilaration of exploration, but Dundry Hill granted us a special perspective. It helped me cultivate an appreciation for nature and a longing for a career in the great outdoors.

My first stepfather was offered an opportunity to work in Bermuda, and the idea of that relocation had excited us all. Instead, he moved us to a characterless urban sprawl of three-bedroom semidetached houses in suburban West London. I was crushed. He chose *this* over Bermuda? Beyond that disappointment, the brutal treatment did not stop, so when he and my mother divorced, I was secretly pleased—and relieved. I loved my mother, but this man was a dark force in our lives. Either we—or he—had to go. She made the right decision. It was not too long before she met another man, and we moved to his London home. The violence stopped. Life improved.

When I first arrived in London, I would cycle for miles in every direction searching for the countryside, but of course, it didn't exist. There were city parks, but in comparison to Dundry Hill, they were dispiritingly unremarkable. The manicured playgrounds and greens were weak imitations of the real deal. As a twelve-year-old, here I was in this ocean of conformity, thinking I'm going in the wrong direction. The school I attended was not known for its academic excellence. Amazing to me now, not a single adult at that time or a single teacher during my entire time at school ever thought to mention that there was a national program available offering free tuition to any university. Lack of opportunity was coupled with an anxiety about the future. In the mid-1980s, at the height of the Cold War, our school forced us to watch the post-apocalyptic BBC movie *Threads*. *Wikipedia* describes it as "[a] film which comes closest to representing the full horror of nuclear war and its aftermath, as well as the catastrophic impact that the event would have on human culture." Looking at it now as a parent, that kind of behavior from a school is insane. The film did little but scare us about what might come.

As I got older anxiety about the future took on a new tone. There were three million unemployed people in the UK. Margaret Thatcher ruled, and people were rioting in the streets. As with my school, it appeared that the government's primary objective was to quash all hope and depress us all to death. The worry was contagious, I was not immune to it, although I also was determined to survive; my teenage optimism was irrepressible. I speculated that the best way out was to join one of the biggest gangs in town—the marines. At age fifteen, in the school career room, rummaging in the bottom drawer of a filing cabinet, I found a crumpled pamphlet. I read the three words that made up the heading—representing the precise inverse of my current situation—*Royal Marines Commandos*. My adolescent mind sparked. From that moment on it was simple, the future set.

The worst-case scenario was nuclear war. I naïvely imagined a post-apocalyptic scenario where, at the very least, as a marine I would be issued a gun, nuclear warfare suit, and a gas mask and have assurances of regular food and consistent logistical and team backup. A dumb kid's lamentable attempt at doomsday prep. A better scenario: there would still be war, but it would not be nuclear. I would get to defend those in need, travel the world, and get paid for it. From the age of eight I knew that the ancient meaning of the name *Alex* is "defender," and my name became a self-fulfilling prophecy.

There was no other choice for me but the marines. When I was sixteen, the marines display team came to the county show. Some of them parachuted in, others fast-roped down from a chopper dressed in combat jackets and green berets. They appeared to kick the shit out of each other in a ferocious, elegant display of unarmed combat, then jumped back in the chopper, and flew back from whence they came—vanishing to a dot in the sky in less than a minute. I allowed myself to blink before I lifted my jaw off the deck. I had never seen men this fit or carry themselves this way. No more comic books—these were real-world commandos, and a wake-up call to adulthood. I fell in love with the corps that day. Joining their team someday became a laser focus of ambition, sharp as a dart in the heart. These men *were* the clash between good and evil, and any other career seemed hopelessly pedestrian.

Finally I felt compelled to leave the suffocating conformity of suburbia. Bulldozers had moved in and razed my school. In its place rose mock Tudor-style "executive" homes. This was the last straw. I had to escape—it felt like my life depended on it.

I enlisted a week or so after my seventeenth birthday, fared well in the nine months of basic training, was promoted to section commander, then had bestowed upon me a Diamond Award—for recruits who achieve a standard of excellence. The commando training was grueling, exactly the right thing for me at the time. The commando's official recruitment tag line was "99.99% need not apply." In the first few weeks of training, we were literally shocked into a new awareness. You either wanted this gig really badly, or you didn't. Most people, quite wisely, didn't.

Each day in training followed a similar format. Up at 5 a.m. Thrashed all day and then crash into bed at 11 p.m. At the outset, during each physical training session in the gym, we would go balls to the wall, maximum effort, then seek permission to puke, and then get back in the gym and carry on. Log runs, mud runs, punishing swims—the pace was unrelenting, and the physical and mental challenges were extreme in comparison to my former cosseted life. The sessions we endured on the bottom field where the assault course was located were called beastings—for good reason. They consisted of sprinting, climbing, leaping, and crawling over, through, and under obstacles designed to stop all progress. The mood in the barracks fifteen minutes prior to a beasting was woeful. No eye contact, no banter, the air filled with wretched dread. Whatever the task that day, the imperative was endurance, and the training team kept us gasping, faces contorted with exertion.

Things got tougher, intensifying week by week. You go through training to become a regular soldier, and then there's the commando phase—a step beyond, which included the endurance course—a very different beast from the assault course. Unlike the foreboding doom we experienced before beastings, prior to the endurance course it was a belly full of butterflies. We smashed through ice to swim through water-filled tunnels, with assault rifles and full gear, only to emerge onto land for more than an hour of wading, crawling, and running. Soaked through and freezing cold, we hobbled back to camp. Some recruits pissed or shit themselves during the five-mile run back. I wasn't exempt. Knuckles would be bleeding from the tunnels crawled through, kit covered with a layer of frost by the time we staggered into camp with clouds of steam rising off our backs.

A school friend who'd successfully completed the course the year before had given me some good advice: "When you need to get a grip," he said, "lock yourself in a toilet cubicle, cry as briefly as you can, dry your eyes, get back out there, crack on."

One in three pass the three-day potential recruits course. Following that, a typical junior-troop-sized intake (composed mainly of seventeen-year-olds) was fifty-five recruits. By the end of training there were usually only twelve left. The contract between the marines and recruits was becoming clear: we will pay you each month, but you need to deliver in blood, sweat, and tears. I was obsessed with completing the course, driven by my covetousness of the prize, the Green Beret.

Our trainers had fought during the Falklands War—including our drill instructor, a keen boxer who took every opportunity to integrate "milling" into our unarmed-combat sessions. He took care to explain the rules.

"Gentlemen, milling is toe-to-toe pure aggression. In a few minutes you will be paired off with an opponent roughly the same size and weight as you. You will have two minutes alone to beat as much blood and snot out of him as possible. If you go down you must get up, otherwise we *will* make you do it again. During the fight you're not allowed to dodge or duck—just take the punches to your face and head and give 'em back even harder!" He concluded by explaining that what they were looking for in each of us was a spirit that was incapable of admitting defeat, the kind that takes a beating and keeps on fighting.

I witnessed several brutal bouts before it was my turn. My opponent stepped into the ring, the bell rang, and the fight began. Defensive tactics were not an option—it was all attack, attack, attack. A massive wake-up call: this was the first time I'd ever been repeatedly punched hard in the face—*bam, bam, bam*—in the space of a few seconds. Forget technique, forget deftness. In a fury I countered, pummeling my opponent's face with a newly acquired savagery. I can still see the surprise in his eyes. The bell rang, the bout finished. Although neither of us was declared the winner, the drill instructor said approvingly, "Now *this* is more like it." My chest was heaving and my face was stinging, and inside my heart was beginning to swell with what must have been pride. This was my new reality, and I was encouraged. I could do this. This was something I could be good at.

Our training sergeant was called Dinger*—our beast-master—and the closest I had ever come to meeting a racist psychopath. One black recruit took heaps of his abuse. This recruit was built like a gladiator, but Dinger wasn't impressed and rode the guy unmercifully. On a troop march in which we were already cracking at breakneck speed, Dinger ordered him to run loops around the entire troop as we ran together as a unit, while carrying a general-purpose machine gun that weighed thirty-six pounds. "Get up here, you fucking black bastard," Dinger roared. "Get that gun and loop around us as we're running. And I want to see your white teeth in your black face, so fucking smile when you do it. Now run!"

Dinger would cackle maniacally as he ordered us to lie on our stomachs with our heels raised and exposed. Armed with a scalpel and

---

*Some of the names within this book have been changed.

bottle of surgical spirit, he relished his task as chief blister lancer. By now, of course, we all had blisters the size of fifty-pence coins, our heels rubbed into raw meat. We squirmed, writhed, and bucked from pain as he applied his grisly "first aid" treatment, and when he was done, he'd insist we'd respond, "Thank you, Sergeant."

We had two Special Forces Falklands War vets in the training team—an officer and a corporal: gruff twins, inscrutable hard-as-nails Scotsmen, both with massive growler mustaches, who were, as Dinger liked to point out, "the cream of British military capability."

One of the commando tests is the thirty-miler—a yomp, or long-distance march, across moorland carrying thirty-five pounds of gear, including a rifle and a shared large rucksack. We had to complete it in less than eight hours. A few days before this test, I woke up in the middle of the night with sharp pains in my back. I got up to look in the mirror and saw that my back was covered with boils, most about half the size of a golf ball. They hadn't been there when I'd gone to bed. I couldn't figure out what they were, but they hurt like hellfire. I went to sick bay the next morning, and the nurse took one look before exclaiming, "My God, what are they *doing* to you boys?" She shook her head, part in disgust, part in disbelief. She was young and new to the unit. Minutes later I was lying on my stomach biting down on a piece of wood that the medics had given me to stop me biting my tongue as they lanced the boils with a scalpel. Triumphantly, one of the nurses pulled from one of the boils a root of white pus that was shaped like a tiny parsnip. Two days later I was back out in the field on the thirty-mile yomp, trudging as fast as I could in nearly a foot of snow across the Dartmoor moorlands.

The entire process of basic training was formulaic textbook military indoctrination. When you begin, you are utterly incompetent. The training team reminds you of this unceasingly because it is true. As a *team* of men we had minimal value. Small achievement by small achievement, we gained competency working together, learning to function as a unit, eventually almost as a single organism. By the time we finished the training, those of us who'd survived felt like titans, omnipotent. This is an institution that *knows* what it is doing. It has an illustrious 350-year history, during which it has fine-tuned the training strategy with devastating effectiveness. Its methods are potent, so potent that many men contribute more than twenty-five years of service.

Punishing as it is, the training succeeds in turning clueless young men with aggressive potential into some of the most skilled fighting soldiers in the world. Though still teenagers, they now, at last, are cutting around wearing green berets, and on the shoulders of their uniforms are patches with red stitching that read Royal Marine Commando. Back when I was seventeen, I had been drafted to serve in 42 Commando, and I had found there a feeling of family that I had never experienced in my personal life. I had served with men twice my age, most veterans of war, and I looked up to them. Those sergeants and sergeant majors became surrogate father figures. They were strong, dependable, fair, funny, and brave. They demanded excellence in everything they did and set a stellar example to impressionable kids like me. I *wanted* them to coach me into manhood, and they inspired me to spend time pondering the qualities of masculinity.

By the time I was twenty, while in the marines in that first enlistment, I had taken the time to finish my A levels, and during my six years in service, I had traveled the world: seeing active service to Northern Ireland and serving in more than twenty countries in Africa, Europe, and the Middle East. After six years I left them to "go outside," as they called it, returning to civilian life. I was twenty-three.

I worked for Guinness for five years and transitioned into a career in IT once the phenomenon of the Internet began to explode into every industry. During these years as a civilian, I felt like I was being infantilized and patronized, especially by aspects of the media. I felt British men were becoming increasingly feminized, emasculated by a culture and lifestyle that was geared toward the needs of women, and we were *embracing* it. I could hardly stomach the cultural and social scam that I saw all around me: I mean, men were being pitched male fragrances, sold the lie that they'd become more sexually successful if they smelled nice! I was not averse to change, especially that of gender roles. Men had ruled society since forever, and now women were having their rightful day in the sun—and who could blame them for wanting that. But men seemed to be losing something intangible in the exchange. Our physical makeup was still the same as it had been one hundred thousand years ago, and while a portion of me yearned for the "caveman mentality," I was aware that in my part of middle England in the late twentieth century, the most dangerous threat a man encountered was scalding his tongue on the firm's cappuccino. That caveman DNA left me with the sense that all was not right in the land of modern manhood. Where was the adventure?

Once on a tour of duty in the Persian Gulf, when I was only twenty, we were between patrols and were sailing through the Indian Ocean, the ship's bow scything through a morass of half a million deadly mating sea snakes. We "parked up," and the captain announced, "Hands to bathe!" He was granting us permission to jump off the highest point of the ship, plunge into the abyss twenty thousand fathoms below, and swim for as long as we dared. Some sailors also steered the RIB (rigid inflatable boat) nearby, using the noise of its motor to scare off inquisitive hammerhead sharks from the pool of shouting crew thrashing in the seawater. Back on board and dry, we sailed off to a desert island for a BBQ on the beach, where we also explored the island or sunbathed before jumping back on the ship and sailing back into the gulf. Within a few hours, under the command of the officer of the watch, I was back on the bridge at the helm, steering the 450-foot-long warship on another counterpiracy patrol.

Now all I had was a cubicle in the city.

In my family men had put their lives on the line, surviving sinking battleships and attacking enemy positions in RAF warplanes. Medals had been won. On my father's side six brothers had fought in the First World War, and only three had returned alive from the trenches. Now I was outside—a civilian in my twenties, running the risk of winning "employee of the month." Surely this was a sign that one man had become another man's bitch.

By age forty life became increasingly comfortable. I was married, with a decent house on a private road, good income, a beautiful daughter, aged eleven, and a fine, headstrong son, aged nine. We had a large shaggy brown dog, chickens laying eggs in the garden cared for by Portuguese gardeners, a Polish cleaner, and a Spanish au pair. But a piece of the jigsaw was missing. Just like the deadening sense of suburban sameness that compelled me to jump ship as soon as I was legally allowed, something drastic was called for to startle me into a fresh, sustainable way of thinking. There was an emerging realization that I needed to embark on a quest.

So after an absence of nearly twenty years, I rejoined the marines as a reservist, a fully trained civilian deployed in times of war. A return to service after an absence that long was unprecedented. Friends and relatives were not happy. Their judgments about my giving up a comfortable civilian life to go back to military service varied from "stupid" to "insane." After all, they said, you have a loving wife, great kids, a chicken called Motherclucker. Isn't that enough? No one supported me. Did I really want to risk my children growing up without a father if I "caught it up" (was killed in action)?

The questions were incontestably justified. Putting things in perspective in the most pragmatic way, I had two main considerations. The first was that in the event of my death, my family would have enough money to support themselves without struggle and to ensure a bright future for the children. I had that covered—there was plenty of insurance to meet their needs. The second concern was how, if I died, the children, following grief, would thrive and stay emotionally healthy. That's a nice way of saying, what would they do without a father? But I realized I also was sure of that, once I stripped out my ego. I trusted my wife—she would find another man who was not an idiot.

My wife didn't find my certainties compelling. She strongly resisted my desire to reenlist, especially with the specter of war looming. We had been married for fifteen years, and she was happy. Why couldn't I be? We argued, but I had never been surer of my decision. We debated the issue for several months, and I'll never forget the night the matter reached resolution. We were sitting up in bed, in heated discussion, and I looked at her and spoke from my heart, with complete honesty: "Baby, I'm deadly serious about this. I love you desperately, and if I come back—and I *will* come back—I promise to dedicate the rest of my life to you and the children. But please, please give me this one year to do this."

After that she never uttered another word of complaint. I now had her support, and I could never have had this adventure without it.

I had met my wife at a friend's party at the Paradise bar near Notting Hill. She'd recently moved up to London from Brighton. Her long blonde hair and get-here-now figure lured me. She was twenty-six and I was twenty-seven, and we spent the next two years together in a flat we bought in central London, then got married and moved out of inner London to a village near its leafier outskirts. Her career took off. She worked at an ad agency in the West End, then gravitated to the city. Before long she became a director within one of the old-guard financial institutions. She knew how to take care of herself, and I could leave knowing she would be OK.

2

The Helmand Candidate

Back in the marines! I spent the first weekend in training abseiling (rappelling) in the dark down a two-hundred-foot office block in a snowstorm in east London. The training team and instructors had all returned from fighting in Afghanistan. Most had also served in Iraq and were ex-regulars. Facing the void, snowflakes swirling in the dark, perched on the precipice and straining forward with only the brake line to stop me smashing into the deck two hundred feet below, Bill, the six-foot, five-inch veteran running the session, asked, "So how long did you spend outside the corps before you came back to us?"

"Twenty years."

"Fair play," he said, then laughed.

I stepped over the edge face first and jumped into the void. The juices were flowing again.

Within a few weeks we were posted to the US Marine Corps Mountain Warfare Training Center in the Sierra Nevada mountains of California. Training was all about navigating, shooting, communicating, and operating effectively at nine thousand feet and above in the snowcapped mountains. We became reacquainted with mountaineering, learned how to ford rivers, and were taught how to pack a mule and three different ways to kill it if we had to. We learned the principles and techniques of close-quarter urban combat, which took place in a town built specifically for the training. The days were long, starting at 5:30 a.m. and finishing at 11 p.m. I was immersed in an epic wilderness and surrounded by men I trusted and admired, who were all equally pleased to be there. Life felt good.

It was a pleasure to be surrounded by real characters, especially old-school funny blokes who didn't give a toss about political correctness. Jenners was a veteran with a West Country burr so broad and deep it felt good down to my bones. He could read out a fire drill and still make it sound as cozy as a hobbit at home in the Shire. For laughs he'd reveal his arse cheeks, exposing the one-inch-deep, two-inch-wide hole in his buttock—courtesy of an RPG (rocket-propelled grenade) attack on his last tour of duty. His post-Afghanistan USA road-trip party trick was to drop his pants in a bar and insert several fifty-pence coins in a neat two-inch cylindrical stack inside the healed hole in his backside in exchange for free beers. He was like a pirate that pops out his glass eye for free tots of rum in an ancient tavern, and it was a privilege just to be around him. When we got some R&R in Reno, he led the drunken cry at 2 a.m. for twenty other marines to go "naked dancing" as the bar was closing. Not a single American in that bar complained. They let the British boys go for it, buck naked on the dance floor until they got it all out of their Afghan-bound systems. No punches thrown or bottles broken. It was good to cut loose. Important. We knew what was coming and that in a few months we'd all be out there.

Thanks to the training methods, everything I had accomplished physically when I was twenty was still doable two decades later. For years I'd been running regularly and in the gym several times a week, and now there was no sign that my body was not up to the task. Beyond the physical conditioning, I spent many evenings and the odd weekend learning new tactics with new weapons. Abseiling, shooting, unarmed combat, mountain climbing, amphibious assaults, yomping (trekking with full kit), navigating—the key requirements and skill set of the modern marine had not changed much, and apart from the odd arched eyebrow from some of both the younger and the more seasoned guys, I slotted back in quickly and without any drama.

The marines immersed me in new *and* risky activities on a regular basis, and I loved it. When we have new experiences, our bodies release a feel-good hormone, dopamine. When we face something risky, they release a stress hormone, cortisol. Those two together are a potent combination, and that's before you include the surge of endorphins thanks to all the rigorous exercise. In an age of increasing self-medication, these natural highs were working wonders. Judging by the faces of the marines around me, this heady biochemical mix was a sustaining daily fix.

For the most part, the men the marine reserves were successfully putting through commando training were older—much older than regular recruits. About half of them had already served time as regulars, and so many of them were well into their mid-to-late thirties. Training and working with them was a real eye-opener. They were not just broiling bundles of testosterone. A significant portion of them were well educated. When we weren't operating tactically, two men in the troop insisted on conducting their private conversations entirely in fluent Spanish. One marine was an architect; another had a PhD in astrophysics and worked as a research scientist at Cambridge University. The troop boss had a master's degree in finance, and my section commander was a thirty-eight-year-old quantity surveyor with two degrees, formerly bored out of his mind by his day job.

Furthermore, *another* marine had a PhD in astrophysics and had lectured at a prestigious central London university. This man, I won't embarrass him by mentioning his name, had to develop a fatherly-like patience with us, as he fielded our ignorant queries into the nature of his civilian work and entertained us with the esoterica of the cosmos during our rare downtime. Our downtime came as we finished a training session, perhaps on urban combat, and the next team went through their training cycle. We'd pass the time amusing ourselves by sitting at the feet of this particular marine-doctor of astrophysics, asking him to explain complex cosmic phenomena in plain language. He'd patiently pitch in with the latest theories in theoretical physics of how the cosmos was constructed or the way it operated. We listened, but most often we baited him: "Explain string theory in layman's terms and in less than ten sentences. Ready? Go!"

Put on the spot like this, he always stepped up, even though we couldn't really understand. It was amusing to experience the contrast between his mini field lectures and the close-quarter battle instructor's training we had listened to only a few minutes earlier, such as the advice he gave about clearing a room. You only exit a room and announce it is "cleared" once you've checked that the enemy corpses in the room are definitely dead and no longer a threat. And the best way to do that is using the eye punch—by poking your thumb into a corpse's eye socket to make sure he is *really* dead. The distance between lethal combat and the subatomic world was beyond reckoning.

Surrounded by this company of men, I felt at home. All of them, despite their educations, had chosen to abandon—or reject—their careers and comfortable lives to take up arms full time and learn how to kill other men for a cause they believed in. Not a choice widely accepted.

Not long after I had reenlisted, the reserve unit I joined was approached by the ex-sergeant major of Zulu Company, 45 Commando. He was a magnetic character who had chalked up twenty-two years of service, two Afghan tours, and an MBE (Member of the British Empire). He announced that the regular marines were asking for volunteers to serve full time on the next deployment to Afghanistan with either 42 or 45 Commando. I was stoked. I did not hesitate for a second to volunteer, and so before I knew it, I was filling in a form for a twelve-month full time contract to serve on the next operational tour in Helmand Province. That same sergeant major was now here in California at the Mountain Warfare Training Center, where one day he gave a speech, quoting words attributed to George Orwell: "People sleep peaceably in their beds at night only because rough men stand ready to do violence on their behalf."

After a year training with marine reservists, we finally got our orders: we were to be close-combat marines in fighting companies in 42 Commando. That was my old unit, from my first enlistment, as a grav (gravel belly—a marine from a rifle company) in 42 Commando. It was like coming home. Within that command I was deployed full time to a regular company, M Company, known as a fighting company composed of 150 marines.

Although I was happy to be "going home" to 42 Commando, my concern was about being accepted by the younger men. I was more than twenty years older than most of them. But I needn't have worried. In the new unit I quickly made friends, among the first of which was a young Scotsman called JJ, a reservist who had been mobilized back into the regular marines with me. We met when we were issued our desert kit, and we hung out together while waiting to be posted to our units.

He was a firecracker. At twenty-two he already had more than five years' service as a marine. He had been everywhere with the corps. His civilian job was as a teacher in a Scottish school, and he loved it—*really* loved it. He had joined the marines as a reservist at age seventeen and had completed his basic training and commando course, earning his green beret at age eighteen while in his first year at university. He had all the attributes that a good Scottish boarding school is known to cultivate: self-assurance, leadership, integrity, self-discipline. Ridiculously, instead of the corps posting him to 45 Commando, which was based in Scotland, he had been posted to 42 Commando, five hundred miles from home. He took it on the chin and became dependent on me for lifts back to London, where he would stay with his father on weekends. His father was the most senior minister in the Church of Scotland and Honorary Chaplain to the Queen and lived in a flat attached to a church in Kensington. For us to get to London and back to Plymouth each weekend was an eight-hour round-trip, plenty of time for us to get to know each other. We'd laugh as he'd tell me about his turns on the dance floor surrounded by his mates, dancing to Dusty Springfield's "Son of a Preacher Man." I'd lap up stories of him carousing around his hometown, Edinburgh, with his university friends. Like me, he had a passion for music festivals, his favorite being RockNess.

Before we headed off to Afghanistan, we had six months' training with 42 Commando in the UK. After that, we would pull a six-month tour of duty "in theater." Pre-war commando training in M Company consisted of icy river swims, backbreaking log runs and lung-ripping distance runs, speed marches in full fighting kit, combat marksmanship, IED hunting, gathering HUMINT (human intelligence), battle tactics, and prisoner-of-war handling.

The fitness regime was harsh, but I had known it was going to be tough. Between my two enlistments, I had the dubious honor now of having been both the youngest and the oldest marine in the unit. The early morning speed marches that went on mile after mile after mile, in groups of up to one hundred men, up and around the infamous Killer Hill, were one of the closest things that the marines have to a psychedelic experience. The perfectly cadenced boots of one hundred men, crunching in unison, became a hypnotic beat that subsumed your sense of self. The subliminal message was: It's about *us*. Together *we* are better and far more powerful than *you*.

At the end of one speed march, I stood in the front row of one hundred men, all of them dripping with sweat, mist rising off their backs. The company commander, private-jet smooth and no spring chicken himself, approached me. He leaned in, peering closely, inspecting the beginnings of wrinkles on my face. He frowned and said, "Fucking hell. How old are you?"

"Forty-two, sir."

He rolled his eyes and shook his head, pinched his nose and blew snot out onto the deck.

"Are you OK?"

"Fine, sir."

I felt better than fine. I still had a choice at this point: I could stick with this outfit or go back "outside," back to closing corporate deals. The endorphins, the camaraderie—there was no comparison. No way was I going back. I was born to do this, in the perfect place at the perfect time.

What's more, this was even better than my first enlistment. Standards had not dropped since the 1980s but had risen. The caliber of the men the marines were recruiting was excellent. These young men seemed to be better listeners and less egotistical than recruits had been when I was last a marine. None of them displayed the old-school hard-man sensibilities just for the sake of posturing. In the late 1980s a lot of the "old sweat" marines had narrow views. Aged nineteen I spent three months living above the Arctic Circle in temperatures often down to −25°F, undergoing arctic warfare training, wearing six layers of clothing, and sleeping in snow holes and a tent sheet. As we sailed home after that training, I had been accosted by some unhappy, heavily mustachioed Falklands War vets. They took umbrage that my hair was too long, saying I looked gay, and threatened to pin me down and shave my head. The irony was that where I came from in West London, their cropped hair and walrus mustaches made them the ones who looked like gay Village People stereotypes. But it didn't matter now. I was surrounded by the new generation. Now the old guard was out. The uber-macho culture that certain marines exhibited in the 1970s and '80s was now practically nonexistent. The young marines still passed all the same tests as former generations of marines had—still delivered the results— but there was no need for superfluous macho posturing. Each man was judged on his actions on ops in the field.

I didn't have much time for reflection. The physical was front and center. The daily runs around Dartmoor's hills were punishing, and I only just managed to keep up with the men, whose average age was about twenty-one. Even the sergeant major was younger than me. Morale was high, and the younger marines viewed me as a curiosity. I felt I could still contribute and add an element of maturity to the team. My progress reports in M Company validated this. We learned to trust each other and worked well as a team, and that was all that mattered. We would be ready for our arrival in theater in "Ganners" (Afghanistan).

Another marine I befriended was Jason, a twenty-nine-year-old who had joined the corps five years previously. We bonded over stories of hedonism and debauchery, spinning dits (stories) about our adventures in clubland. I was pleased to have found a kindred spirit. Essentially, he was someone who could distinguish between fulfilling his duties within a dedicated military life and enjoying the downtime. We both liked to dance and party. He was a good bootneck (marine) and exemplified the core attributes and ethos listed on the marines website: unselfishness, determination, good sense of humor, cheerfulness in the face of adversity, high physical fitness. He had it all.

He told me stories about his first tour in Afghanistan. Once, in a mountainous area, a NATO unit, which shall remain nameless, came under attack by the Taliban. Back then, tactically, the Taliban were much more willing to attack en masse in the conventional sense of close combat, even though they were hopelessly outnumbered and outgunned, many of them using ancient rifles and rusting weaponry. Describing the lopsidedness of this battle, Jason said, "It was like the Ewoks fighting with bows and arrows against Imperial storm troopers." Instead of a lone Taliban gunman being gunned down, as was typical by 2011, previously much larger groups of enemy died when they engaged. But the element of the story that most struck me was that some troops had become so enraged during the battle that in the minutes after combat, one or two of them went around smashing in their dead enemies' heads with bricks and rocks. Killing them with bullets and grenades wasn't enough—those Taliban had just tried to kill them, and they weren't getting off that lightly just by dying. As uncomfortable as I felt by this, I also imagined the Taliban doing the same to the marines—and to me—if the tables had been turned. I didn't realize how naïve my judgments were then, as it wasn't long before we all discovered that what the Taliban were doing was cold-bloodedly worse.

The recruiting copy on posters and billboards around the country reads: "Royal Marines: It's a State of Mind." The inference being that having the correct state of mind will enable you to accomplish what you set out to do in life—in this case to survive and win in battle. Although I was fully a marine in body, heart, and mind, I also was not one-dimensional. Far from it. Unbeknownst to any of my marine commanders or buddies, I was a keen explorer of states of mind that were the antithesis of military culture. And that is the flip side of this story.

3

Infinite Insight

This *is the secret that can't be told.*

TERENCE MCKENNA

In the 1960s and '70s, people took psychedelics and became anti-war. Not me.

I started altering my consciousness using alcohol. Who hadn't? By the time I was twenty-one, I'd been drinking for four or five years. Plymouth's notorious Union Street was a haven for men seeking a drunken night out. Violence broke out almost every night when everyone spilled out of the clubs. I was no different and got into fights. In retrospect, none of them would have occurred if alcohol had not been involved. Nine times out of ten, the violence was caused by somebody's ego being bruised, so that person felt he had to defend himself or attack.

By 1989 ecstasy had become popular in the bars and clubs of Plymouth and London. Strangers smiled at and hugged each other in chemically induced waves of warmth and affection. Although I explored consciousness-altering substances as a civilian, it wasn't until I was almost forty that I first smoked DMT as a white powder made from the roots of *Mimosa hostilis,* an Amazonian DMT-containing

27

plant. The experience came a couple of years before I reenlisted and was called up to Afghanistan. On the Internet DMT was often called spice. The mind-expanding, and some might say mind-blowing, effects last only eight or ten minutes, but that's long enough to change your life. After one short, spellbinding experience, my entire view of the world changed—and much for the better. More importantly, my view of death changed, too. In fact, the shift from fear of death to a belief—a certainty—that our souls, or consciousness, survive physical death was a significant contributing factor in my decision to go to war. DMT, or rather the reality I experienced through using it, prepared me to face my own death. Some might call it a spiritual awakening, but I'd define it as a consciousness awakening.

I had heard of DMT back when I was twenty, having read about it in *i-D,* a UK magazine. I made a mental note then that if I ever got the chance to try it, I would. Back then, pre-Internet, information about and access to DMT was rare. But twenty years later it seemed to be everywhere. There was a lag of a few months between finding an opportunity to try it and actually taking it, and during the interim I did some research. The Internet was a trove of information, although decidedly mixed in terms of accuracy and reliability. Some of the sites or video clips about DMT had been viewed more than three million times. Things had really changed over the past two decades. One book in particular held my attention. It was by an American researcher who in the mid-1990s was one of the first to receive US government approval to study the effects of DMT in a clinical environment. It was called *DMT: The Spirit Molecule* by Dr. Rick Strassman.

With the proper dose, set, and setting, DMT is safe, and I was psychologically prepared to experience it. I was with two good friends, one of whom acted as our guide. David warned me that I was about to experience one of "the strangest, most perplexing, confounding, incredible, mysterious, mind-boggling, and amazing substances known." Using DMT, he said, was serious business, not something to undertake lightly or recreationally. "This is for the serious seeker," he explained, "although you won't really understand until you do it." Explaining some of the science behind DMT, David also told us that one of the reasons the DMT experience felt so natural was because DMT (N,N-Dimethyltryptamine) occurs naturally and endogenously as a neurotransmitter in our brains.

The three of us were tucked away in a safe location in a rural log cabin. After I made myself comfortable on a large, brown leather beanbag, David loaded the recommended quantity into the pipe. The advice was to lie back, close my eyes, and relax. Purportedly, three hits on the pipe is the magic number, so three hits it was. Breathing the first one in, I held the smoke in my lungs for eight or nine seconds, exhaled, and then repeated.

I'd barely let out the second inhalation when my vision started to dissolve; I had just enough time to take in the third lungful before everything I knew and understood about the real world completely transformed. The next several minutes changed my life forever. In the space of a few short seconds, I was shot—cleanly, smoothly—out of this dimension and into another that was beyond comprehension. Leaving the confines of my body, I was no longer bound by three dimensions; I was tumbling into a void that rapidly morphed into the most spectacularly beautiful sight I had ever seen. Colored lights swirled kaleidoscopically through ever more dazzling geometric shapes, which propelled me through the universe at warp speed, approaching the speed of light, entirely alert, completely lucid. After a minute or so I found I could, to some extent, control the sublime vistas by changing the focus of my thoughts, all the while remaining fully cognizant. After about two minutes I had the unshakable sense that I was not alone. I had moved beyond the colors and geometric shapes into a different space, full of sentience, sensing a *presence* that hinted at an infinite and boundless love, possessing an awesome intelligence and power. *Is this God that I'm experiencing for the first time?* I felt safe, protected. *This* must be what it feels like to be dead. At one point I had resigned myself to the fact that I actually was dead and wouldn't be returning to my body or Earth's 3-D existence. But it didn't worry me—I was glimpsing heaven. My ego had been utterly vaporized, and an entirely new aspect of consciousness was made apparent. I became aware that my left-brain rationality had put me in a semidormant state for my entire life up until this moment. *Is this what it feels like to be truly conscious?* The third eye of esoteric lore had blossomed, burst into life with the brightness of a lighthouse in the very center of my mind, revealing me for the first time as a soul-being, as opposed to a thinking rational human.

As the intensity of the visions and feelings diminished, I remembered the DMT-related advice given by Terence McKenna, a wildly original thinker and author of many books about entheogens: "Pay attention!" and "Try not to give in to astonishment!" Laughably easier said than done. Even while undergoing it, I knew this was one of the peak experiences of my life, that I was yielding to a transformation, an awakening, believing for the first time that I was witnessing a genuine miracle. Now I understood wise men who had said, "Not only is the universe weirder than we suppose, it is weirder than we *can* suppose."

I also knew that when it came to judging what is real, to a large extent I had been wrong for my entire life. Up until this point, a momentous breakthrough, I had known the world only through the lenses of rationality and science. But DMT revealed how intellectually stunted the position is that says if something can't be measured, it doesn't exist. Through DMT I saw how unquantifiable reality is. The keys to throw open the doors to the mind are all around us in the natural world, and we have only to *want* to insert the right key into the lock of the door of perception. I felt the world as sentient right down to its core. Over the years, growing up and embracing the material-realism of our culture, I had ceased to believe in any kind of God, having worshipped at the proverbial altar of rationality and empiricism. But now DMT had blown that certainty to smithereens and replaced it with a new kind of surety, a metaphysical and spiritual one. I had felt the presence of some sort of overmind, an undeniable kind of God consciousness.

All in just seven minutes.

It had felt like an hour, and the experience of coming back to our consensus reality was as pleasant as the rocketlike blastoff into hyperspace. I was called back to Earth by one of my friends clearing his throat. The sound broke the spell, and I suddenly realized I was back in my body and sharing 3-D space. But I wasn't quite *all* the way back. I opened my eyes. Every object in the cabin was enveloped by gorgeous geometric colored patterns. As my "spirit" settled into my body, I felt relief. But more than that, I was filled with awe for the world and with love and compassion for everything in it. Initially, I didn't want to speak. I *couldn't* speak. I was emerging from an experience where my ego had been smashed, and paradoxically, it was a sweet liberation. Words could never convey the profundity of what I'd just felt and witnessed. The prospect of my life one day ending forever in the finality of death was now absurd. The way he was looking at me, I could tell that David already knew this and was waiting patiently for me to assimilate the insight. When I did speak, I had no real capacity to express what I meant. David had given this gift to me, and I was so overwhelmingly grateful that I was brought nearly to tears.

"Thank you so much. I am so, *so* grateful."

That was it. Otherwise I was stunned into silence. I just kept shaking my head in absolute wonder—finally I understood what *real* astonishment was.

David smiled and accepted the compliment. He knew the experience was profound. This was not like standing on the edge of the Grand Canyon and saying, "Wow, this is big." This was way bigger than that. I felt as emotional as when my children were born. To be given these insights—that we are not alone in the universe, that there *is* life after death, that our consciousness does not reside isolated within our brains and skulls—was the grandest and most compelling epiphany. The experience left me ready to face the possibility of my own death during war. The sacred revelation of an afterlife once our meat jackets expire was a priceless asset in preparing for Afghanistan and, just as importantly, coping with it while I was there.

This first encounter with this "spirit molecule" was so profound that I had absolutely no compulsion to repeat it anytime soon. I needed time to integrate that first experience. Growing up, like millions of other people, I'd spent countless childhood hours singing hymns, learning about the spiritual teachings of the Bible, and occasionally attending church. Yet, all of this enforced religious activity had had zero effect on making me spiritual in any sense. All that time and effort spent by other people trying to teach me how to be a religious believer had been wasted. And now, incredibly, all it had taken to flip the switch to turn me from an agnostic to spiritually aware was three inhalations of an exotic compound in a log cabin. The perception of a higher intelligence, the *presence,* was real. It was inconceivable that my prosaic brain could manifest anything approaching this complex and stunning beauty. I wanted to just be with these insights, and so it would be many months before I felt ready for a second encounter.

The military policy about drug taking, particularly imbibing psychotropic substances, was basically that "hallucinations would not be tolerated under any circumstances." If a member of the military was ever caught taking recreational drugs, especially those that induced hallucinations, the consequences were severe—imprisonment and dishonorable discharge. If such substances were caught even in the possession of a serving military person, then the likely penalty also was imprisonment. So, clearly, a serving member of the UK military was not to alter his or her consciousness using psychedelics—or presumably any other method— under any circumstances.

In the marines the only acceptable types of hallucinations were the ones experienced when the body and mind were reaching their absolute limits, pushed almost to breaking by training, or while under the duress of actual combat operations. I had once experienced mild hallucinations under such conditions, and other marines I knew had too. A twelve-hour mountain yomp at night—bearing a heavy load and enduring extreme exertion—could do it. We'd swap stories of livestock that wasn't really there, nonexistent taxis on mountain sides—all kinds of ridiculous things that an exhausted mind can conjure up in the wilderness. It happened often enough that it was thought to be nothing out of the ordinary. As a marine, if you had a physical task to complete, you pushed yourself to a level of exertion that made you puke and, if required to get the job done, hallucinate. The corps expected this display of commitment and determination. They even encouraged it, because some day lives would depend on everyone contributing that kind of extreme effort. But as for the use of natural consciousness-altering hallucinogenic plants, they were considered no different from other illegal substances—lazily and ineptly categorized as just another kind of drug.

Controlling the use and access to any kind of mind-altering substance, from alcohol to hallucinogens, in a military environment while troops are on active duty makes perfect sense. No one wants to put lives at risk or compromise operational effectiveness. However, there may be a place for these substances therapeutically. In 2011 the *Daily Telegraph* reported a university study publicizing clinical evidence showing that some of these psychedelics diminish anxiety, help relieve post-traumatic stress disorder, and can reduce the fear of death. If any one class of people feels stress, anxiety, and fear, it is combat troops. But it was taking time for the law to catch up with the new data. I came to believe that these substances could have a useful place in the military if used in the proper set and setting, under controlled conditions. Now, more compassionately in the United States, they are starting to explore their use to treat PTSD in returning war combatants. But to my knowledge they have not explored using them beneficially to help their own troops self-actualize, to confront fear and death, *before* they engage in combat. There is no pre-war ritual for this, although I think there might be a place for it.

I was aware of the contradictions in my life and value system. I saw purpose in natural entheogens and their ability to open us to the exploration of transcendent realms, yet I also chose to undergo one of my culture's life-defining tests—war. I am not so different from thousands of other men who seek out such tests. And there are others who yearn for it but never do it. The unfortunate reality is that in the twenty-first century, there are few opportunities for young men to undergo a real rite of passage into manhood. Women have childbirth, but there are no male equivalents. Speaking from experience, winning a rugby tournament, closing a big business deal, or delivering a public speech doesn't come close to being such a rite. Most men my age grew up hearing all kinds of hair-raising stories from World War II of derring-do and self-sacrifice in the delivery of service to your country in the fight against tyranny and evil. That kind of patriotism had changed complexion with more recent wars, such as Vietnam, Iraq, and Afghanistan, but combat experience in particular remained a central and singular rite of passage.

When I reenlisted I wanted to discuss the use of psychedelics with other members of the unit but was convinced they did not know about or had never had an experience of psychedelics, such as DMT and psilocybin. While I did not use consciousness-altering substances as a marine—I would have never put myself or others at risk by doing so—I could not even openly seek out these kinds of conversations, so I kept my opinions to myself. My two desires—serving during a war and exploring my consciousness with psychedelics—stood in stark opposition. The marines had a binary outlook on the matter since there were only two states of consciousness they valued—alert and asleep. The mantra "stay alert, stay alive" was never far from anyone's mind while we were training for deployment to Ganners.

David had been appalled by my decision to go to Afghanistan—actually, he was utterly disgusted. He had spent three years trekking through nearly fifty countries in Asia, Africa, and South America. We each had traveled to over thirty countries and had a perspective wider than our own culture, and our conversation turned to the topic of whether malevolent forces are in control of Western democracies.

For most of our lives, our country and others, particularly the United States, had instigated—or done little to avert—warfare. Now with the "war on terrorism" and the "war on drugs" (David called it the "war on consciousness") stoking patriotic fervor to preserve our way of life and defend ourselves against zealots and madmen, it seemed unlikely that we would ever stop. David espoused the view that the military intervention in Afghanistan was part of an insidious wider strategy to maintain power and subvert developing nations to perpetuate the Western political status quo and further the aims of rapacious Western corporations. By serving in the military, I was participating in a dishonorable conflict, naïvely manipulated into doing the dirty work of the world's baddest bad guys.

My rebuttal was that "evil prevails when good men do nothing." We had invaded and toppled the Taliban, and so we had to take responsibility for what came next. What were we supposed to do now, leave this place alone like a festering sore? Everyone knew that two of the primary sources of motivation toward terrorism are poverty and ignorance. I was sure that one of the most effective ways Afghanistan could claw its way out of poverty was through universal education. Under the Taliban regime, girls were not allowed to go to school. In 2008 alone there were nearly three hundred Taliban attacks on schools, including bombings. Hundreds of children were being killed and maimed, when all they were doing was showing up at school. Imagine the uproar if even *one* school in our society was blown up by terrorists. This very thing was happening somewhere in Afghanistan just about every week, and most of these attacks went unreported. Any country that limits itself to educating only 50 percent of its population will, by comparison to other nations, always remain economically deprived. Since the Taliban regime was toppled in 2001, more than two million girls had been able to attend school, but there still was by no means equality in the genders when it came to education.

"Isn't the education of two million girls and millions more in the future a decent cause?" I had argued. "Don't girls have immeasurable value? Consider the contribution that two million additional educated minds can make to an impoverished society."

My appeal to logic fell on deaf ears.

Were we being manipulated by forces of rapacious self-interest and evil? One of my best friends had just accused me of playing into the hands of the dark masters. I had listened and countered, but I couldn't help harboring some doubt. I had thought more than once, When you're on your way to war, you'd better be batting for the right team, right?

So, I had to go there and find out for myself. My direct experience would help me determine what was true. David's friendship and my love affair with entheogens would be taking a backseat. I had other more pressing things to focus on as I prepared to join my unit. I was now one of them—a Taliban hunter on a mission.

4

RULE NUMBER 1

Don't Shoot Your Mates

The training momentum of 42 Commando accelerated. Regular intelligence briefings provided news about threats and the intensity of operations in the areas we would inherit from the Parachute Regiment. Our AOs (area of operations) had been assigned, and we were fed news of incidents occurring on a weekly basis in our assigned patches. The reports were not encouraging.

It was sobering to learn of the casualties. Our briefing room was covered in maps highlighting shootings and detonated IEDs. Every piece of available data was scrutinized. Violence was systemic. In the area to which we were about to be deployed, two soldiers had been killed by a single sniper bullet—a freak incident, or bad luck, rather than the application of a professional sniper's skill. Nevertheless, that single bullet had passed through the head of one soldier, exited, and then passed through the neck of another soldier. Stay alert, stay alive.

We had been split into multiples, teams of sixteen to twenty-five close-combat marines. Each multiple was responsible for patrolling a few square kilometers of territory within the province, and ours had been assigned a district within Nad Ali South, near Lashkar Gah, the capital of Helmand Province. We would patrol in support of other teams that flanked our territory. The profile of that province did not instill confidence. The minister of education in Helmand was illiterate. So was the chief of police. A documentary TV series crew who had followed L Company's exploits in Nad Ali had christened the area "the most dangerous square mile on Earth."

Death began to haunt us like an unwelcome companion as we completed a ghoulish set of predeployment tasks. Each man was required to write both his own eulogy and a last letter that would be delivered to his family in the event of his death. DNA samples were taken so that we could be indentified if our corpses were unrecognizable. I tried to resist some of these requirements, but was "volun-told" to comply.

What no one ever tells you about the marines is that to get to Afghanistan you have got to fight just to get out there: complete nine months' basic training, six months' predeployment training, two weeks' acclimatizing training—fail any of the weekly tests along the entire way and you *will* be binned, barred from playing with the big boys and toys in the desert. Our first stop en route was Camp Bastion, a vast military city built in the desert and home base to thousands of the British forces and the forces of several other ISAF (International Security Assistance Force) countries. It included an airport with runways long enough to accommodate any type of military aircraft and a leading-edge medical facility. Our company—M Company—was quartered in huge tents. They were cramped, dark, and dusty: temporary billets for eighty men, who would sleep in the rows of iron bunks. We had two weeks to acclimatize and train before deploying to our patrol bases and forts. There was no hope of escaping the heat. We arrived in April, and the temperature was already 115°F in the shade.

The Ministry of Defence now categorized our status as "in theater"—their dark euphemism for where drama happens. Our attitudes had changed as drastically as the landscape. Lightheartedness vanished. The civilizing influence of women had waned now that they had vanished from our lives. Outside the tent marines were peacocking, aggrandizing about fit models and fat chicks they had fucked—and how. The bravado spoke to the sweet times of the past to counterbalance the hardship ahead. Slowly the testosterone tap had turned from a drip, drip, drip—to a gush. From a perch on a top bunk, I peered through the gloom at dusk to survey the scene. Eighty men and their gear were crammed in the tent, after having spent another day on the hot firing ranges zeroing weapons. There was no personal space; every available inch was jammed with tired, dirty bodies. Hundreds of weapons were laid out for cleaning: assault rifles, sniper rifles, Minimi light machine guns, 9-mm pistols, general-purpose machine guns (GPMGs), bayonets, commando daggers, Leatherman knives and tools, KA-BAR fighting knives. Body armor was stuffed full with grenades, magazines, and ammunition. Exotic thermal imaging and infrared telescopic sights lay around like grotesque exaggerations of conventional optics. Adding to the jumble of weaponry were medical kits, tourniquets, morphine syringes, radios, batteries, headphones, and microphones. Add to that rucksacks, patrol packs, and desert high-top combat boots. Everything was shrouded in gritty dust, including us. That did not obscure the evidence of readiness: everybody was honed to the peak of fitness, and the majority were festooned with tattoos in all kinds of designs and colors. We were trained and seasoned—and I pitied anyone with the balls to try to engage us. Motivation was high. Many of these men—some barely more than boys—had waited their entire lives for this mission. We had wrung every last shred of physical and mental effort from ourselves to get this far. These men were among the cream of Britain's young men, and it was a privilege to witness the scene. Not many people get to see marines preparing for war, and I soaked it up. Many of the marines were on their third tour of duty yet still only in their twenties.

Long before we got here, we had all known that the cost of this tour would be paid in pain and distress, and perhaps even with our lives. Our sister unit, 40 Commando, had lost fourteen men during their last trip to Helmand, and many more marines had been seriously injured. Everyone knew the odds, and we trained hard to defeat them.

We retrained in a close-quarter battle compound clearing and spent hours firing grenade machine guns and antitank weapons. We listened intently to countless lectures on how to detect different types of IEDs. We took refresher courses in battlefield medicine. We were counseled on how to withstand the extreme heat and to operate in a hostile environment. The threats came not only from the Taliban but also from poisonous insects and nasty infections. Nothing about this land seemed friendly, and we were taught to assume everything was potentially deadly.

As we ticked off the days until heading into the field, a new kind of tension developed, one barely perceptible but somewhat akin to the sensation of static electricity. Banter took on a serious edge, even an aggressive and adversarial one. For example, a common announcement prior to playing an iPod playlist on the speakers in the tent would have been something like, "Lads, listen to this, you'll love it." But something that simple gradually morphed into, "Anyone doesn't like these tunes can fuck off." Our insults became uglier: the everyday "knobber" or "cock" was now a "fucking prick" or worse. An old derogatory label that had been dished out forever in the corps was to call someone Jack, as in "I'm all right, Jack" (sod everyone else). It referred to selfishness. Our lives depended on the team. As deployment day neared, the term *Jack* got bandied about with increasing frequency. Everyone was aware of the subtext that every man must always, always maintain the healthy cohesion of the group. So, complaints like "He's Jack" and "That's Jack as fuck" were heard with increasing regularity as men became less patient with one another. It didn't take long for rule number one to become "Don't be Jack."

Other changes were in our level of attention and ability to listen. We made sustained, unbroken eye contact, we communicated with increased concentration, our focus became paramount. Every communication conveyed the unspoken message: "I understand what you're telling me, and I want *you* to understand that *I* am listening very carefully and realize that our shared understanding will keep us both alive."

Miscommunications and mistakes could kill us—even here in training. One event proved how cruelly true that was. An hour after we had finished a live firing session, an army regiment stepped up to train in the same position. During a mock assault on a compound using live ammo, a young soldier somehow—perhaps he tripped—shot his friend in the head, not once but twice. His teammate's helmet stopped the bullets from penetrating his skull, and he was able to walk away, dazed and severely pissed off. We were dumbfounded. How does a man accidentally shoot his mate in the head—twice?

One evening we were sitting around waiting for full darkness to fall so we could complete a night shoot on the range. We passed the time playing poker. A sandstorm erupted, the wind scattered cards everywhere, and the world became bathed in an eerie light, an odd reddish hue. There was no place to get out of the storm, so we became our own shelters. We covered our faces with *shemaghs* (Afghan scarves) and instinctively closed ranks into small groups, facing each other until shoulders were touching, our backs against the viciously whipping sand and only our eyes visible in our swathed heads. This became an unspoken tactic for dealing with these storms. Jason affectionately referred to these circles as "rings of steel." Good luck trying to penetrate one as a late entrant—there was no getting in. Dust devils whipped up a frenzy from the desert floor, spinning vortexes rising three feet hight, like tiny perfectly formed mini tornados. Energized by the roiling desert forces, the men's voices would ratchet up to full volume as would their energy—the effect was electric as they sparked off each other, telling dits and joking. The atmosphere was absolutely bizarre, the desert and all of us at full-blast status. But it was just another moment in a marine's life. We could add withstanding sandstorms to scaling mountains, sailing oceans, trekking though jungles and deserts, and burrowing into snow holes in the Arctic.

5

Peace Be upon You

We jumped on a chopper to fly to our patrol bases to get out on the ground at last. My multiple, 43 Bravo, was assigned to relieve the Paras—the Parachute Regiment—in a fort called Zamrod positioned on the edge of a village of approximately three hundred people twenty miles away. The exhilaration of flying in a Chinook in the desert with the tailgate down can't be denied. Men bristled with bullets, bayonets, and guns. The roar of the rotors made it impossible to hear speech, so everyone was forced to lip-read commands shouted their way. The chopper flew low, swooping and banking to minimize exposure, much like an extreme theme-park ride, only this one could get you shot out of the sky at any moment.

Below us the desert was flat and featureless, giving way here and there to irrigated farmland, dotted with mud compounds. We landed at M Company HQ and disgorged from the chopper into seventeen-ton armored Mastiff vehicles for the final short leg into Fort Zamrod, arriving at the start of what was known as "fighting season."

Once in Zamrod, the novelty of occupying a fort was short lived. The Parachute Regiment multiple that we were relieving was still inhabiting it. They all looked gaunt, particularly their sergeant, the multiple commander, who looked like the actor Tom Berenger (without the facial scar) in the movie *Platoon,* although his Yorkshire accent ensured the comparison ended there.

We spent the next two days in a formal handover process, listening to the local intelligence gathered by the Paras. Naturally, we sucked it up, as our lives depended on it.

The first patrols went smoothly, and we got a feeling of the normal pattern of life. All senses on high alert, vigilant. We may as well have traveled back in time five hundred years, as the area was practically medieval. We were especially vulnerable when forced into tight spaces or channeled. Men became alert to known Taliban aiming markers, looking for ground sign, anything unusual and unnatural—suspicious wires, disturbed earth, metal objects. Close attention was paid to atmospherics. The mantra "absence of the normal, presence of the abnormal" played over and over in our minds.

We patrolled through the fields, and opium poppies grew everywhere, blossoming with pink and white beauty. Farmers harvested them as the most normal crop in the world. For them, of course, it was. Initially it was incomprehensible. During his first exposure one of the lads piped up, "Hold on, hold on, wait up, settle down a minute, everyone, please. What the hell's going on? What the fuck? Can you see all this shit? This takes gangster to a whole new level. This stuff is *everywhere!*"

"Wake up, dummy," said one of the old sweats. "Governments have always done this. Same shit, different war."

No one could move a few meters outside the wire without traipsing through opium poppies, which grew up to our chests. Dried poppy heads crunched under size 10 magnum desert boots. Spread throughout Helmand, elite troops from different countries were securing, guarding, and nurturing the industry that produces 90 percent of the raw material for the most destructive drug. Certainly these poppy fields benefited from government-sanctioned protection. Was this a part of the war on drugs or war *with* drugs? It has always been like this in one form or another. There *was* more to this conflict than meets the eye. David would have a field day. We were supporting this community, ensuring their well-being, while they cultivated crops processed into heroin. Quite simply, we were in new territory as a military mafia running shit on a new turf. It's no accident it's called the military industrial complex. Nothing random going on there.

Never get high on your own supply. I wondered if anyone had broken the golden rule out here?

The adult men in the villages had deeply craggy faces with thick beards, looking ancient and wizened. The male villagers were either very old or boys. All the able-bodied men were dead or off fighting—with us or against us. We hardly ever saw any female villagers. They weren't allowed out of their houses without a chaperone.

On most patrols we wore and carried the following kit:

- trousers, UBACS (underbody armor combat shirt), belts, and high combat boots
- antiballistic protective underwear
- antiballistic groin protector, aka "the nappy"
- body armor, which included a large twelve-inch front plate, a similar back plate, and two smaller side armor plates
- Kevlar helmet
- assault rifle fitted with an ACOG (advanced combat optical gunsight), red-dot laser light, and LLM (laser light module) UV/black light
- plenty of SA80 assault rifle magazines containing 5.56-mm rounds
- high-explosive grenades
- bayonet and/or commando dagger
- smoke and white phosphorus grenades
- backpack containing an eighteen-by-twelve-inch steel ECM (electronic countermeasures) device fitted with a brick-sized battery, plus a spare battery
- personal radio, microphone and headphone, and spare batteries

- eye protection antiballistic glasses
- NVGs (night vision goggles)
- one set of personalized ear defenders
- multiblade Leatherman knife, with pliers
- black Protrek wristwatch with compass, altimeter, and thermometer
- bandanna
- kneepads
- headlamp
- medical pouch containing two syringes of morphine and assorted dressings and bandages appropriate for gunshot and blast wounds
- two tourniquets primed and worn in an upper-arm pocket applied in the event of a catastrophic hemorrhage
- three liters of water in a CamelBak (a water pack with a hose that snakes up your shoulder, close to your mouth, enabling hands-free drinking)
- a life-saver bottle (a three-liter water-purifying container)
- two ration pack meals
- weapon-cleaning kit and spare oil
- waterproof notebook, pens, pencils
- dog tags
- biometric camera equipment

This kit had to be serviceable before every patrol, each piece tested and checked as operational. Fully loaded, a typical patrol kit weighed between 110 and 120 pounds, and it had to be humped hour after hour every day in 115°F heat in the shade. And the shade always, always seemed to be elsewhere, tantalizingly elusive, wherever we weren't. It was fucking merciless.

The compound walls at Zamrod formed a square, with each wall eighteen feet high and five feet thick, constructed from Hesco mesh-wire blocks filled with sand and rubble. Stout enough to stop a rocket-propelled grenade. At two of the corners, opposite each other, were sangar towers (elevated sentry posts that provided an unobstructed view of the surrounding terrain). There were sixteen marines in our multiple, and we all rotated sangar duty. Each tower had to be manned 24/7, which meant we pulled guard duty all the time. The sangar towers were our early warning system of attack. The local Taliban could attack at any time and in a variety of ways: suicide bombers in vehicles or on foot, grenades lobbed over a wall, snipers shooting from local compounds. Every one of these threats had materialized into real-life horror stories.

Our accommodation was two tents: olive green and canvas, with space in each for eight marines and their gear (one rucksack and one shoulder bag as a maximum for each man for the entire tour). There were camp beds, each with a mosquito net. I considered the cots a luxury, having spent countless months on exercises over the years in the field with just a foam roll mat to sleep on. But that's where the luxury ended. This was home for the next six months, and immediately we discovered, with devastating disappointment, that the tents were impossible to spend more than ten minutes in between the hours of 9 a.m. and 7 p.m. due to the heat. During the day, if it was 120°F outside the tent, it could get up to 130°F inside. Instant sweatbox.

A third tent was used for "welfare." In it were two battered-looking laptops with the odd key missing and an intermittent wireless Internet connection. Facing the communal TV were a couple of makeshift sofas creatively fashioned from wire, covered with blankets. We discovered that a sofa made from thick metal wire could never be made comfortable. We also shared a kitchen-eating area, commonly known as the galley to marines, that was little more than wooden posts holding up a corrugated tin roof. There was rarely anything to mix together to cook. Our food for the next six months was a daily (twenty-four-hour) ration pack, of which there were about ten different menus. Each ration was a ready-made boil-in-a-bag affair, and they quickly lost their appeal. Even with the ten different menus, after we had been through one rotation, we cursed the monotony. Same food, same menu, week after week for six months. Men became alchemists trying to spice up meals, but there was no turning lead into gold. No fresh meat or vegetables. No dairy. No milk, except occasionally in powdered form.

Communal jobs—the housekeeping tasks—were divided up among us, usually with two men assigned to each job: cleaning the galley, shower area, and welfare tent and emptying the crap from all the toilets. We crapped into plastic bags called John bags, which were then dumped into larger black trash-can liners and burned with petrol along with the rest of our gash (rubbish) every day.

Standard operational procedure dictated that we strive not to patrol according to any set pattern, which impacted the timing and how and where we patrolled. Consequently, there was no routine for the duration of a patrol or the time of day it went out. Patrols went out day and night, typically averaging four hours. When not patrolling, there were plenty of other things to do, including manning the sangars. With only sixteen men in the fort, we each typically spent six hours a day manning a sangar. We developed a system of two hours on sangar duty, then six hours off. A typical day started with a patrol at 6 a.m., usually until about 10 a.m. Even on the shortest patrol, we would come back exhausted, drenched with sweat. Then we'd either work two hours of sangar duty or have two hours of admin time—personal time filled with laundry, cleaning our kit, and preparing meals. The pattern repeated: back out on patrol, back in the sangar, admin time.

This regime played out day after day, for the entire six months, and was, to be frank, demoralizing. Imagine a life where on Friday, the next day is Monday. The whole fucked timetable was compounded by the fact that there were no days off whatsoever, so every day was Groundhog Day. Days of the week and weekends became utterly meaningless.

Typically, men never got more than four hours' sleep at a time, five if they were exceptionally lucky. In addition, all hope of any downtime for meditation or rest was snuffed out by the constant clatter and seventy-decibel judder of a hulking diesel generator, killing the aspiration on day two. So sleep, and the lack of it, soon became an all-consuming preoccupation. I'd often leave to go out on patrol at 1 a.m. and return at 5 a.m., getting only three hours in bed before being awakened for rotation on the sangar—which never ever, ever went away.

Worse still, we had to wear full body armor and a helmet while in the sangar, whether it was day or night, and the heat was beyond oppressive no matter what time of the day. Sangar duty became our curse. Inescapable, like taxes and death.

Bish was a twenty-two-year-old, wearier than his years. This was his second tour, and he was no stranger to the rigors. During his previous deployment, he had had a brush with a suicide bomber who had unhelpfully detonated his load only a few meters away from where he stood. Bish had to pick bits of the bomber's flesh and bone off his weapon and uniform. Whenever he relieved me on the sangar, I could always hear him approach. He would climb up the stairs saying, "I hate my life, I hate my life, I hate my life." So much for maintaining the marines maxim of "cheerfulness in the face of adversity."

We were owned by the military with no autonomy. We had no control over where we went, when we slept, whom we worked with, what we wore, what we ate, the workload, or its duration. The machine had us by the balls, and we all knew it. Our only mechanism to vent frustration was swearing, and we swore and swore—and then swore we'd never come back here. I tried to keep my dripping (grumbling) to a minimum. Everyone had volunteered, and we had gotten what we'd asked for.

It took only a few patrols to learn that it took an astonishing level of exertion to complete each one. With all the weapons and kit, the heat was brutal. Everybody rapidly lost weight. Sweat ran off our bodies the moment we started to get rigged for patrol. The only way to stop a river of perspiration flooding your eyes was to wear a bandanna, which became soaked through and sopping wet within two or three minutes of getting kitted up.

We had the agility of tortoises. Commando training taught marines to be agile, focusing on deft athleticism and speed. These attributes were now sacrificed to meet the demands of combat effectiveness while attempting to optimize safety. Wearing body armor made sense and saved lives, but the price we paid was in agility. Medieval knights in suits of armor had more freedom of movement than our sorry limbs did. *Disgusting* was the word some of the younger marines used to describe how they felt during the long patrols. Staying fully hydrated was essential but impossible. No matter how much water I drank, my piss was always a dark amber brown.

On patrol the local children chased us endlessly, shouting "Chocolate! Chocolate!" We'd respond with the customary *salaam alaikum* (peace be upon you). The kids wanted the boiled sweets that we carried in our ration packs. We would throw them by the handfuls, like a shower of confetti. The children would scramble and scuffle, fighting one another to grab them and gobble them down. It never ceased to amaze me how bold these kids were. If the patrol halted, you'd find some cover, drop to one knee and assume a firing position, covering your arcs of fire. When we did this, the kids had no qualms about reaching out and actually unbuttoning our combat trouser pockets in an effort to fish out sweets. Countless times children tried to remove my watch from my wrist. When they got obnoxious we were tempted to slap them away, but we had been warned not to, or do anything that could be misconstrued by the villagers as abuse. Some marines had booted pesky kids up the arse, and it had not gone down well with the village elders. They filed assault reports that had been fed up the chain of command, and the whole incident had led to bad vibes between the community and the troops. Incidents like that could undo many weeks of building good-will. Luckily, sometimes the children's own elders intervened, disciplining unruly kids themselves. The punishment usually was brutal and immediate, fathers and grandfathers slapping and beating their children in front of us.

Many of the children could never be regarded as optimally healthy. I was shocked at how many children were boss-eyed and cross-eyed. The custom was that villagers marry within their tribes and wider family. Inbreeding was obviously rife, the poverty endemic. Some children had open running sores on their faces and limbs, and they seemed completely unfazed by the writhing mass of flies that covered the sores. I gave a young girl a boiled sweet, and she smiled in thanks, and a few of the young marines with me recoiled, wincing as a black trail of assorted insects marched out in a neat line from her nostril.

One day an old man approached, and Gabby, our interpreter (terp), relayed his request: "When you get shot at, could you please try to show some restraint with your guns?"

The last time there had been a firefight nearby, three villagers had been killed. He understood, he said, that we needed to defend ourselves but begged us to not use grenades and antitank weapons when we were attacked and especially not when we had to breach the doors of houses in which suspects may be hiding. Gabby tried to reassure him that the level of our response would be appropriate to contain the threat and keep us alive.

The old man went on. If we knocked on doors with the intent of entering their compounds to make arrests of suspected insurgents, or to search for weapons and bomb-making material, to please give them plenty of time to hide their womenfolk. It was extremely important, he explained, that the women be completely out of sight of male strangers; if they weren't then this would bring tremendous shame upon them—both the men and the women. It brought home a sad truth. This kind of patriarchal dominance really does exist. In our culture—in the businesses, schools, governments of Western societies—what would happen if women were not allowed to leave their homes unless accompanied by men? Society would grind to a halt. Gabby said he was tempted to condescendingly respond: "Sir, perhaps you might reconsider this ancient belief that your culture has imposed upon you. Does it really serve your community well?" Fantasy, of course. He relayed his real response, "Of course, sir. We'll comply with your request."

Our interpreters, native Afghanis, were worth their weight in gold. Most of them were well educated and lived in the fort with us. They accompanied us on every patrol, a vital linchpin between us and the communities for which we were providing security. Their job was not only difficult but dangerous. They faced vicious reprisals for helping us from those who felt they were at best collaborators and at worst traitors. Their identities were kept secret, because if the Taliban commanders discovered their real identities, they were murdered.

Speaking through our terp Gabby, an elderly man told us how grateful he was that we had come to protect his community. He understood, he said, that all the men in our patrol had flown thousands of miles and left their families behind to come here to protect his own family and village. His words turned out to be the only kind words I ever heard from the local Afghans.

It's not like soldiers or marines expect to be thanked. Such thanks, if they were expressed to anyone, were most likely directed toward Yoda, our sergeant. He ran the *shuras* at our fort. Shuras were weekly meetings held with the local village elders to discuss security matters. Often, friendly farmers would bring us information of insurgent intimidation, although we couldn't accept that intel at face value. Many of the locals lied about Taliban activity in the hopes of cashing in, believing we'd pay cash incentives for providing intelligence. We never paid for information. But that didn't stop them from trying. We began to recognize the worst offenders and turned them away before they could even begin to plead their case. But good information was crucial, and the shuras were a place to get it.

In addition to running the shuras, Yoda had full responsibility for the day-to-day running of the fort. He was entrusted with the welfare of all of the marines. He had one of the hardest, most stressful jobs in the world. Aged thirty, with a killer intellect, he had to do everything the younger marines did physically, but he also had to plan and lead our day-to-day operations, both within the fort and outside it. He was responsible for enforcing standards and discipline—not easy, always walking a tightrope. I didn't envy him in the slightest. We felt lucky to have him. He'd completed tours previously in Afghanistan and Iraq. This was his third on the front line, and from the beginning I knew he was extremely capable and intelligent. If he wanted to, Yoda could have done almost anything in any profession. He was extremely quick witted and had an excellent knowledge of how the corps operated. I was happy for him to lead. I'd already made the decision many months before to park my ego and let more experienced men take charge. For too long my civilian job had wrought stress of a different kind. I was here to help protect the local population from insurgents, watch the backs of the marines in my team. Simple . . .

Opium Blues

Two weeks in to our tour, we had our first KIA (killed in action). I was in the sangar and heard a formidable explosion to the east. An IED had exploded and struck a patrol from L Company—my original old company. A young marine lost both his legs, and although the medics tried their best to save him, he bled out on the chopper back to Bastion.

One of the men, on his third tour, married with four kids, said, "I came into this world kicking and screaming, covered in blood and guts, and that's exactly how I'm gonna leave it." Clearly, I wasn't the only one who, prior to getting here, had seriously contemplated the likelihood of dying here. If you do, the stress diminishes massively.

As we walked out for the morning patrol the next day, I was last man out. As he closed the main gate behind me, Taff—one of the older guys, exceptionally diligent and altruistic—said, "Be careful out there today."

"What do you mean?"

"Some of the blokes went back to where the IED killed the marine from L Company yesterday. When they got there, they found body parts strung up in the trees by the Taliban to taunt us, hung out like trophies. Remind the lads that if they do find pieces of anyone's body lying around, don't touch them—they'll be booby-trapped. It's how those paras got killed a few months ago. Same kind of evil."

"You serious?"

"Deadly."

"Jesus fucking wept."

The gate closed behind us, and I was on the wrong side of it. If you're not completely paranoid, then you're not contributing to the team. Paranoia is a virtue here, especially on night patrols. Many nights, usually between the hours of 1 and 4 a.m., we'd stake out the compound of a suspected Taliban commander. We'd patrol up almost silently, then use night vision optics to get as near to the target as possible in the pitch-black darkness. We'd used the same tactics in Northern Ireland. Once we had eyes on the target, we took turns rotating the surveillance equipment, keeping watch for nefarious activity. The slightest sound would set dogs barking, so the rules for survival and success were no light, no noise, and, once we were in position, no movement. After several hours, satisfied that all the right intelligence was fed back, we'd extract silently and patrol back to Zamrod.

One time, in total darkness, we crept around the wall of a compound and had gone to ground to take a two-minute breather. A villager came out and crapped in the stream outside his house. He had no idea that he had eight sets of eyes boring into him less than fifteen feet away.

Everyone was suspect. Guys would train their red-dot laser sights on the backs of oblivious local men who came within a few meters of our lay-up point until they were satisfied that the men weren't Taliban out laying IEDs under the cover of darkness. They were usually just innocent workers padding home after irrigating their fields.

Daytime patrols were no easier. After an arduous seven-hour patrol in 115°F heat—I had been carrying the heaviest ECM kit and by three in the afternoon had drunk seven liters of water in an effort to stay hydrated—a local told us that the previous night the Taliban had planted a bomb on Two Hundred Street, a heavily populated street less than three hundred meters from our fort. We positively ID'd the device, at least ten kilograms of explosives planted specifically to target

43 Bravo. Yoda called in the EOD (bomb disposal) team, and they detonated it safely, causing a huge explosion. It was an eerie feeling knowing that your personal daily movements were being closely tracked and a concerted effort had been made to try to kill you. No one else from our unit came around here. That bomb was specifically set to target me and my friends.

The root cause behind the IEDs and sniper fire was deadly beliefs. People on both sides of the conflict were dying as a consequence of these beliefs. The same night of the KIA, while on sangar duty, I was given a lecture by a devout Muslim. Gabby was visiting his family for a few weeks, and so another terp was filling in. I hadn't yet learned the new guy's name, and I knew he didn't know mine, but now here we were sharing the sangar tower. He knew he had me cornered. Unprompted, he launched into a speech, with complete sincerity and an attitude I can only call devout, about the truth and superiority of Islam, claiming that most of the innovative technology that millions of people around the world enjoy had first been written about in the Koran, back in the seventh century. Islam, thus, had incredible foresight, which was yet another reason why Islam was, in his words, the "one true religion." With wide-eyed earnestness he suggested that I seriously consider becoming a devout Muslim—right away, today even. His reality bubble plainly was very different from mine. As this joker rambled on proselytizing, I thought, Why do so many Christians and Muslims want to convert everybody to their way of thinking? What is it about these desert religions that makes them do this? Haven't they heard of, or understood, the meaning of tolerance? Can't we just be different? Do they realize that if I invented Christianity from scratch today and then tried to get people to believe me and follow this new religion tomorrow, how ridiculous I'd sound?

The new terp fell silent, smiling inanely, obviously waiting for a response. Considering his words for the tiniest fraction of a moment, in that sliver of time I thought many things: It was the middle of the night. I was still working after a long, hot day of patrolling. The threat of being blown to pieces, day in and day out, was a real concern. Extremism and fundamentalism had brought us to this godforsaken province in the first place, and now this man was trying to convert me. This was bullshit. I nearly grabbed him by the scruff of his raggedy Afghan neck and launched him twenty-five feet out of the sangar tower, headfirst. Luckily, fate stepped in, and he was suddenly called away to the other sangar to interpret the request of a farmer whose land bordered the fort. Just as well, because I knew the shit-for-brains wouldn't have liked my answer.

Ahead of deployment, anticipating the generation gap between me and my team, I attempted to generate some social value to integrate as innocuously as possible. To boil it right down, I offered material bribes. I brought two team hammocks, money to play poker, new music (courtesy of DJs Pete Tong and Annie Mac), several sets of iPod speakers, a Solargorilla charger for everyone's iPods, and two hundred quality movies loaded onto a hard drive for communal use with each man's laptop. Several American HBO TV series were loaded onto various digital memory sticks (*The Sopranos*, *The Wire*, *Breaking Bad*, *Game of Thrones*, *Entourage,* and *Modern Family*). The episodes were often watched back-to-back by the men in between patrols.

Inevitably, I fell into something approximating a surrogate dad role for some of the younger men. During downtime between patrols, I'd have one-on-one's and offer alternative career advice over a coffee to these disgruntled grunts who were trying to seize back some semblance of control in this mire of adversity. I felt obliged to remind them of their good characters, give them encouragement that they'd succeed in their future roles outside, out of the marines. When you have no control, you get thirsty for options. I was touched to see how modest and insecure some of the lads were about striking out, making their mark outside the military. Bish wanted to be an ambulance paramedic but was sure that he wasn't good enough, despite his real-world experience as a combat medic, a first-class assault engineer, and a stack of good A levels. He sat crumpled on his canvas camp bed, morosely staring down at his battered boots, as I said to him, "Trust me. After serving two tours out here on the front line by the age of twenty-two, armed with the qualifications you've got, you *will* be taken seriously. For fuck's sake, you've had to scrape bits of suicide bomber off your face as part of your service to your country. You *have* to have faith that you can do it, mate. People *will* put their trust in you. Jesus Christ, if I was hiring for the role and you were a candidate, I'd hire you in an instant!"

Others in their early twenties were bright and quick witted with aspirations to go into business but had few qualifications. So I'd try to coach those that were interested about how to acquire the skills and experience to earn a consistent six-figure salary, ethically, within five years. But what I couldn't guarantee, of course, was whether this would make them happy. Some listened attentively; others weren't interested at all.

Taff was twenty-nine and keen to know how getting married and becoming a father would add a new dimension: Would it really be worthwhile? Lee was our corporal and his son was just two years old, and so he wanted to know what he had to look forward to as a father to an older boy. I ventured that all young boys really just want their fathers to *be exciting*. It struck a chord, and he nodded thoughtfully.

The sergeant major would pay us a visit every few weeks, give us an operational situation report, and piss everyone off by telling the marines to shave their beards off. Once business was concluded, the real business began. He had a knack for finding every man's insecurity, sticking a verbal knife into it, and turning the blade slowly. He had the impeccability and wit of a professional overtly in control: he *owned* every scenario he was embroiled in. Mere rank was a preoccupation for mortals; his charisma transcended it, effortlessly trumping all the ascribed hierarchy, an unmatched master of man management. I couldn't help but shake my head and smile in private admiration.

I once read that sleep is the opium of the soldier, and this is true. I woke up one morning dreaming that I was on patrol, bringing up the rear as tail-end Charlie—the last in formation. I heard gunfire and instinctively ducked. Slowly, the sound of gunshots got louder and louder as the enemy approached our position. Then I awoke from the dream, startled. I *still* heard gunfire. J Company was coming under attack again to our east. The sounds of the gunfight had invaded my dream.

Gunshots and the crump of artillery were constant. Later that day while on sangar duty, I saw two Apache helicopters attacking some compounds to our east, their fearsome guns spewing death and carnage. Dust and rubble rose up from the explosions. As they circled around and around their target, they looked like two huge deadly vultures.

By late May, Gabby was in need of another morale boost. With increasing frequency I heard him muttering, "I want to go home." He missed his family, and within the next few days, he was lucky enough to be granted leave. He was relieved by Dashim, a muscular twenty-two-year-old. He settled in well, had lots of energy, and was always smiling. We became friendly, and he soon referred to me as his brother, despite the fact that I was old enough to be his father. He was one of twelve children, his mother a physician and his father a senior officer in the Afghan army. Because he was from an educated family and well educated himself, having successfully studied for and obtained a degree from a university in Kabul, he was significantly Westernized. Convenient for us and exactly the kind of man we needed.

But he hated Helmand. He held an open contempt for the locals for whom he was tasked to interpret; he viewed them as ignorant and bigoted and considered himself urbane and civilized. He often referred to the young men who tried to trade information—usually always false information—for cash as "fucking lying bastards." His English was that good.

He loathed the Taliban as much as we did. He held strong opinions about them: their methods, objectives, and long-term strategy were all part of an intellectually stunted worldview. He knew full well that because he served as our interpreter, he was considered to be a traitor by many of his countrymen, and he felt that if he didn't have our protection, within ten minutes of leaving the fort he'd be captured, tortured, and shot. When I asked him why he became an interpreter since it was such a risk, he said that he wanted to do some good and to stand on his own two feet. He'd moved here from Kabul, which is just about the only thing he talked about with real fondness, and had aspirations of bettering himself. He sought respect from his family. Based on his backstory it was easy to see he had family issues to resolve, that it was important for him to bring honor to his family and, vitally, receive it from them as he matured. He spoke of the time he was working in a barbershop, and one day he'd smoked opium before beginning to work on a customer. While clipping the man's hair, he spotted a beautiful woman passing by in the street.

"I fell instantly in love," he said.

But instead of approaching her tactfully with a smile or asking someone for an introduction, he abandoned his customer midhaircut and ran after her. When he caught up with her in the middle of the busy street, he somehow, and for some reason I could never fathom, grasped her, forcibly bent her over, and tried to insert one of his fingers into her rectum. As you might expect, this scene ended badly for him. The woman shrieked and screamed, and the police were called. To compound matters she was a fully qualified lawyer and now a most displeased one. Dashim was arrested in full view of his boss and all his customers. His mother had to come down to the police station and bail him out. He admitted that it had been mortifyingly embarrassing. I didn't doubt that for a second, as I nearly fell over laughing. No wonder he felt the need to regain his family's respect.

He was right about the risks of being an interpreter employed by the ISAF. Terps faced exactly the same dangers as the troops they accompanied, and many of them were killed while on duty. Verbal threats followed them wherever they went. There was a very real risk they would be assassinated while home visiting their families. Their job also put their families at risk. For these reasons and others, the identities of our terps were closely guarded secrets. They, and we, never used their real names. There were plenty of occasions where Dashim was subjected to abuse from local teenagers and young men. They'd call him a traitor and the Afghan equivalent of a fucking wanker. Naturally, these insults upset his normally cheerful character. I did my best to reassure him that he was doing a good job in difficult circumstances.

As much as I liked him, he was a mystery. I had difficulty reconciling that this cheerful, hardworking, and educated young man could also be brutal to his enemies. Prior to working with British marines, he had worked as an interpreter for the US marines. He told me what he had once done to a prisoner. The Americans had captured a Taliban fighter who had been shot. He was badly wounded and writhing in agony. Dashim looked so proud of himself when he told me that he'd bent down and castrated him as a reprisal for his attempt on their lives. He said everyone around him had laughed their heads off as he'd done it.

7

Best Man's Grief

It was June, and there was no variation from the cloudless blue sky and unrelenting sun. Comedian Bill Hicks's rant about the weather in Los Angeles played again and again in my mind.

"I hate it," he said. "It's hot and sunny every day. Hot and fucking sunny. Every day."

We were landlocked; the sea was at least another country away in any direction. Even the "river" wasn't real—it was a channel scraped out of the desert, a superlarge irrigation ditch serving the runoff from mountains so far away they weren't even visible. People grow up and die here for generations without ever even seeing a mountain, a river, or the sea. Every feature is man-made, every piece of vegetation planted.

That said, most local men *did* have plenty to eat, plenty of children, several wives, and access to unlimited free opium and cannabis, which grew wild by the bushel.

On patrol, to lighten the mood, Matt, one of the lads from the Reconnaissance Troop (Recce Troop) told the boys following us begging for sweets that his name was Cock and Balls. We all soon adopted this moniker, and smiles spread across our weary faces when we heard the kids shout "Cock and Balls! Cock and Balls! Cock and Balls!" as they tried to pry sweets from us. For the rest of our tour, it wasn't too difficult to pinpoint where 43 Bravo was on patrol during the daytime—all you had to do was stop, listen carefully, and before long you would hear the children singing out, "Cock and Balls!"

I asked Matt a question, as we shared a cigarette after a postpatrol debrief with a group of other guys. "Where do you get your confidence from?"

"Dunno. S'pose it's just innate. I was bullied by an older kid when I was little. He used to steal my shoes on the way to school, and I had to walk to school with no shoes on. We were pretty poor. My dad had an MBA in finance, but instead of going into business, he lectured at a university. My mum didn't work, so it was always a struggle. I bumped into the bully once after the pubs shut, walking along the canal with my girlfriend. I'd been in the marines for a couple of years, but this guy didn't know—we hadn't seen each other since school. Anyway, so this cocksucker's walking past me and says something out the corner of his mouth, sneering, drunk, stuffing kebab in his face. So I just banged the fucker out, battered him with one punch—*smack*—straight under his jaw. He flew straight in the canal with bits of kebab floating around his head."

Everyone laughed. Ah, revenge. I mused . . . so base, so primitive, so sweet. It was great to have him there.

The next day on patrol I heard the massive crump of an explosion erupt. Matt and I looked at each other, wincing, and waited for the orders to jump into our gear and get going. Smack in the face news came that JJ had been badly injured by an IED. He had been searching a compound suspected of being a Taliban bomb-making factory. The same IED had killed two marines and badly injured two other men, one of whom was an Afghan interpreter, who later died of his injuries. That left only four marines alive in JJ's patrol to deal with the casualties, the dead men, and any remaining threats in the compound.

Oliver Augustin, a young lieutenant, was one of the men killed. Another was Sam Alexander—the best friend of Jason, my friend in 43 Bravo. Jason had been best man at Sam's wedding. They'd been in basic training together and had been sent to the same fighting company in 42 Commando. They spent most weekends together and DJ'd on a local Internet radio station. Jason had badgered me to listen to their radio show before we got out here, and they were good. Sam had already been awarded a medal for bravery during a previous tour. He was a hero and left behind a wife and young son.

My heart wrenched for Jason. Over the course of the tour, I had watched him take so much unnecessary bullshit, and he didn't deserve any of it. He was given only an hour off duty to grieve. When he returned from R&R, he had Sam's name etched in an elegant design in a tattoo on his forearm.

Information trickled through. JJ had severe fragmentation injuries to his legs, one of his arms had been smashed to bits and part of the elbow was missing, several fingers had been severed from his other hand, and one of his eye sockets had been fractured and crushed.

That night on sangar duty, I couldn't get my mind off JJ's injuries, brooding over how the children he taught at school might treat him. I hoped they wouldn't be too cruel about his disfigurement. I wondered how he'd deal with it all in the long term. He was always so upbeat, but now I worried that this personal disaster might change that. Not being able to see JJ was a test of my patience.

Not having contact with my own family was hard, although it was by choice. We had access to free secure mobile satellite phones, but what was I going to say to my wife, kids, parents? Life here is shitty. The food is crap. The heat is brutal. Friends are being killed and maimed—and for what? So I decided to write home every couple of weeks instead of call.

Yet still, I had no doubt that some of us were out here to try to set the record straight. Before being mobilized I considered all the human suffering caused by dictators, despots, and tyrants—history's worst, the atrocious, loathsome shame of men. Time to fight back. Restore justice. And who really knew all the causes of 9/11? Collectively we reap what we sow. But we had to get real and face the fact that the men who *we* had voted into power had brought us here—and now we were all dealing with the consequences.

One thing we could have confidence in was that we owned the night. The Taliban were using older technology, forced to use ordinary white-light torches to navigate in the dark, making them easier to spot, and so they generally avoided operating at night. In contrast, we had night-vision goggles (NVGs)—which made all the difference. Men looked like part mutant cyborgs while wearing them. It was eerie patrolling in the pitch black using NVGs, with everything bathed in a grainy green light. Dashim said the locals called us ghosts because we had a habit of materializing at night, seemingly from nowhere. We also had laser light modules (LLMs) mounted on our personal weapons, an infrared torch that assisted us with navigation in the dark.

Although our technology kept the Taliban threat to a minimum at night, it raised the risks in other ways. While wearing NVGs we couldn't easily detect the ground signs that alerted us to freshly laid IEDs. It became just a matter of time before the senior command decision to patrol more at night led to our unit's first nighttime casualties. Marines started getting blown up by bombs they could have avoided during the day. We began to seriously question the value of these night-time patrols. The Taliban weren't around, but their handiwork was. The official position was that at night we had ground domination and could deny the enemy freedom of movement, but that reasoning ignored the trade-off: deaths and catastrophic injuries. That decision was a bitter pill to swallow, especially if you were the man on the ground.

Patrolling one night we saw a small Taliban unit about three hundred meters to our south in an irrigated potato field. The younger guys were desperate to open up and engage, but Yoda was against us blazing away because of the risk of civilian casualties. Unless the Taliban engaged us first, it was thought to be too rash to shoot to kill without proper qualification. So, instead, we put up some schermuly night flares to illuminate the ground and patrolled toward them. By the time we got there, they'd disappeared. Bollocks.

Don't Think

Three months in and I was not the only one thinking that some sort of psychosis would manifest unless we got some decent sleep. Our body clocks had surrendered in confusion weeks earlier. Another typical day: up at 2 a.m. for two hours of sangar duty, then 4 a.m. go on patrol, returning at 10 a.m., my back hurting so bad I had to swallow 800 milligrams of ibuprofen. Then admin duties and more sangar, until it was time for patrol again from 5 p.m. until 10 p.m. Take care of my kit and fall onto my bunk for some shut-eye until 4 a.m., when it was time to go back on the sangar.

I fantasized nearly every day about what luxury it would be to spend the rest of the tour in an English prison: temperate climate, full night's sleep, TV, bed with a mattress, three cooked meals a day, no backbreaking physical labor, no chance of being shot by a sniper. English prisoners were lucky bastards.

A friend sent an article from the *Daily Telegraph*. A senior British army officer complained about the operational effectiveness of ground troops being compromised by the sheer weight of our gear, the ammunition and weapons we had to carry on every patrol. The 120 pounds seemed ridiculous. My children didn't even weigh that much. Even in the Falklands War over twenty-five years ago, men had marched with 80 pounds of gear. Seemed like we were going backward.

After a few months I got into a routine of finishing a patrol, attending the postpatrol briefing, and then enjoying the highlight of the day: a lie down on a six-foot-long, two-foot-wide ripped-up cardboard box that I had carefully positioned in one of the few shady spots next to the ops room. I'd retire there for an hour with my Kindle. Other men did the same, often claiming one of the few covetable medical stretchers, each man competing for the slithers of shade dotted around the fort. I developed an affection for that dusty, shitty piece of cardboard, like a dog retreating to the sanctuary of his basket.

Irrigation ditches ran around the villages, and as we waded through them, turds drifted by our thighs. Human crap was everywhere because there was no sewage infrastructure. Often I'd drop to one knee next to a compound wall taking up a fire position and then get hit by an overpowering stench. A cursory glance could reveal six or seven turds within a few feet. Tactics techniqes and procedures (TTPs) dictated that we never advance in set patterns and that we alternate our routes wherever possible on every patrol in order to minimize any predictability that could be exploited by enemy snipers. The net consequence was that we had to wade through filthy water every day.

Our uniforms stank. We had to hand-scrub them every other day at a minimum. We'd hang them to out to dry in the sun, and within a couple of hours they were baked rigid, impregnated with so much sand and dirt they could be folded like cardboard. Each man had only two or three liters of water a day to wash clothes, and our do-it-yourself detergent was a splash of shower gel, never enough to properly clean a uniform. It just seemed to wet the material and muddy the water. Even after my uniforms were washed and dried, I could still feel the grainy dirt embedded in the fabric, and they retained their cardboard texture. To say that marines take pride in their personal cleanliness is an understatement, so being forced to live like this was another little chiseled dent in morale.

We never had cold water to drink in Zamrod—I was in the field for two months before getting hold of a bottle of chilled water, and I had to walk for three hours to get it. We had patrolled up to Khammar, the company HQ, and discovered they actually had a couple of refrigerators that really worked. It was unquestionably the best drink I ever tasted! Heaven delivered in a little plastic bottle. At Zamrod we had a solar-powered fridge, but it didn't work because it was missing a crucial part—the solar panel. The fridge sat there month after month in the galley, a hunk of dumb metal, mocking us. So we'd had no cold, or even cool, drinks at all for at least five months. It *cannot* be underestimated how much we take cool water for granted. At home you turn on a tap and it's just *there*. Here we had no running water, and with no refrigeration, all of our bottled water was ambient temperature. Since this was Afghan summertime, that meant the water was always warm, and by the end of the day, it was often far too hot to even sip. No exaggeration—it was scorching. Each evening men scavenged around the fort for a bottle that had been in the shade long enough that the water didn't burn their tongues when they took a sip. When you come in from a patrol, covered in filth, exhausted, completely soaked in sweat, the thing you want most badly in the world is a long, cool drink of water, but even this simple pleasure evaded us. So, the chilled water I got at Khammar was liquid bliss. I drank half of it and poured the other half over my sweaty and dusty head, shivering with pleasure.

When we got visits from other teams in M Company's AO, inevitably it became a ritual to swap stories about the rudimentary living conditions in the respective forts. We engaged in competitive one-upmanship, comparing complaints. At Khammar that day, one of the visiting corporals told me that his fort actually had a clean freshwater stream running right through it. The water came up to their waists, and after the patrols, they would strip off and wash in it. My bullshit radar was on high alert. He must be lying through his teeth. I had to verify his story. It was true, and I was mute with envy, imagining that if we could just have this one simple luxury at Zamrod, then everything in my world would be OK.

Midsummer's day—my birthday. I received a few packages from my family. The main presents were a bottle of 400-milligram tablets of ibuprofen painkillers from Julia and three liters of orange squash. Perfect. Relief from both body aches and the monotony of drinking warm water. The sergeant major sauntered past me as I opened a bottle, commenting blithely that I looked skeletal. I wouldn't have known. The mirrors here were no bigger than the palm of your hand.

Normal took on a new meaning, both in the fort and out of it. We were patrolling through a small village, and we could sense something was amiss. Although we were unfamiliar with this area, the village was a ghost town. "Absence of the normal, presence of the abnormal": if it feels weird, be on guard. We were on high alert as we closed in. It felt so eerie that it almost seemed like a staged setup, an atmospheric cliché. *Something's happening, the shit's gonna hit the fan, I can feel it . . .*

Taff spoke the words everyone was thinking, "This fucking place is creeping me out, man."

As we snaked around one of the outer compounds toward the surrounding deserted fields, we took incoming fire from the south. Sniper! Everyone dove for cover. A quick visual check revealed that none of the lads had been hit. Most of us took cover behind the same wall. Yoda launched a smoke grenade and ordered the sharpshooters, whose weapons had more powerful telescopic sights, to move through an irrigation ditch out to the flank to see if they could get eyes on the enemy. A young boy working in the field realized he was caught between us and the sniper. Terrified, he started wailing and crying, running as fast as he could, calling out for his parents. He was the same size as my son. As he ran toward safety, we turned away, scoping the terrain for the likely enemy firing position. A sharpshooter was next to me, and we both edged around the wall, covering the south. He dropped to the ground on his guts in a ditch in the time-honored gravel belly position. A man was out there somewhere trying to kill us, and because of that he deserved to die—right now. Our eyes lingered on every potential firing position, but none of us spotted anyone we could positively ID. The lone gunman survived.

News filtered in that American SEAL commandos raided and killed Osama bin Laden. Naturally, we stayed put. Excellent news, but it was not going to end the war. The biggest manhunt in all of history was over, and now we needed to mop up. To compound things we heard that five hundred Taliban prisoners had escaped from prison in a mass breakout and were now at large—*again*. Well that's just fucking great, just what we need. How many men gave their lives trying to catch those men in the first place? Imagine that happening back home. Heads would roll.

I went to bed and listened to the crump of explosions. Mortars, IEDs, grenades—it was hard to tell which was which, but each time the image was the same in my mind, a marine losing his legs in the worst carnage imaginable. With an increasingly childlike attitude, night after night I'd lie in my bunk and ruminate on our predicament. Why can't I get a day off in months? How's it fair that I get to carry the heaviest piece of iron on practically every patrol? Who decides that I get the shortest amount of downtime between a daytime patrol and a night-time patrol? What is going to mentally corrode first if I continue to get less than four hours of sleep a night? When will we ever get a cold drink or fresh food? *Sweet baby Jesus, just shut the fuck up, you jabbering Muppet.*

Conventional problem-solving thought, the relentless internal dialogue, would not help me now. After months it hit me, salvation from the incessant internal rant, the sweetest insight: Don't think. Don't think. I learned, like an Indian sadhu, to repeat that mantra over and over until I literally stopped thinking and the quiet mind arrived. Repeat "don't think, don't think, don't think" hundreds of times, and all of a sudden, guess what? You're no longer thinking. The sweetest relief, and then sleep's sweet embrace. Thank the Lord, I had found a coping mechanism. Just as an obsessive-compulsive's ritual grants him or her some semblance of normality, this mantra gave me non-sense, no sense. Stop sensing, censor the senses. My own mind is the source of my distress, so detach from it and find peace. I realized I could use this for the rest of my life.

The next day Yoda briefed us to be on the lookout for two teams of Taliban suicide bombers in two white Toyota SUVs. "Fuckers have joined a death cult, and they don't even know it," said Taff, shaking his head bitterly. "Haven't we all," said Yoda, smiling.

9

Back in the Game

One of the terps handed me a handful of raw, untreated, compressed opium. He kept it in a John bag to mask the smell. It looked and felt like dried grass. The opium was the size of a man's fist, and no doubt if consumed in the right way, it could last awhile—although I really didn't have a clue. I'd been given a stash of drugs in the middle of a war zone. What would you do? Temptation flashed momentarily. Who hadn't been tempted? Isn't a pimp tempted to sample his stock? My weary mind mused that if refined opium resin was good enough for illustrious British gentlemen colonial explorers, then a gift of this weaker, unrefined kind from a well-meaning terp was worth contemplating. After all, the British Empire had started, funded, and engaged in open warfare during the Far Eastern opium wars in the nineteenth century with the full intention of selling it wholesale to the Chinese. So our global credentials in the war on drugs were impeccable.

If the terp, or any man, were caught with drugs, he would face an indignant authority figure playing out his public role, no doubt slotting in the word *disgrace* somewhere during the disciplinary process. We all knew that. What serviceman's mind had not gone down this rabbit hole? We all wanted pleasure. You could self-manufacture all the endogenous opioids you want with exercise and exertion—but smuggle any back that was nurtured in the poppy fields we patrolled, well, not so good.

I handed the bag of opium back to the terp.

Every human has the sovereign right to control his or her own mind, providing of course that no one is harmed. Although with opium, let's not tiptoe around it—the risk of addiction must be taken into consideration. When it comes to psychoactive substances, psychedelics are my preference. Opium and its harder derivatives are a diversion, useful to mask pain, as evidenced by the morphine that we carried on every patrol. Opiates *contract* consciousness, whereas psychedelics *expand* it. Millions had cottoned onto this in the sixties, and for me expansion is the name of the game. Exploring alternative states of consciousness is good, but I'd stuck to a self-administered ban on using any mind-altering plants while still serving. We had wised up to the fact that the forty-year farce of the war on drugs initiated by President Richard Nixon was part of the deal here, but being *at* war *on* drugs was out of the question. But if you *were* an aspirational smuggler and ever did want to get it back, how would you achieve this undetected? If we were to envisage a purely hypothetical scenario: some terps occasionally emigrated to the UK, and if one of them *was* interested in taking it in, it's likely it would be a one-off—no chance of any resupply. Meanwhile, I asked the terp how they consumed the drug.

"Simple. Just soak the plant fibers in boiling water, dip a cigarette into the oil that skims the surface, let the cigarette dry, then smoke it."

R&R back to the UK came in June, halfway through the tour. The Chinook flight from Khammar back to Bastion started with a rush of exhilaration. We swooped and banked across the desert with the airframe's tailgate down; the door gunner alert, huge black visor covering his face like a character from a sci-fi movie. I was excited to be going home during Glastonbury, a music festival. I would have a week with my family before heading off to the festival, then return to spend every minute of the rest of my two weeks with Julia and the children.

At Brize Norton airport, in the UK, 150 troops disgorged from the aircraft. As soon as we entered the baggage hall, sniffer dogs—trained antinarcotic dogs—clambered over us. Dogs meticulously sniffed each separate pocket on our trousers, no one escaping intimate canine attention. They sniffed around every rucksack that came off the plane, as well as all the handheld bags. This would not have bode well for anyone's private opium-den aspirations, regardless of whether you were a traveling terp or a hypothetical scenario spinner.

The relief of seeing my family was immense. As a belated birthday gift, Julia bought me a session in a flotation tank—the most effective way to propel you into a psychedelic state without the actual ingestion of psychedelics, the perfect warm-up for the next big event. Several days later I headed to my umpteenth Glastonbury Festival, a summer indulgence where, along with 170,000 others, you could leave your identity and cares at the main gate. It is a fantasyland of sublime hedonism. I was determined to obliterate any thoughts of Ganners, immersed in the now as each special moment unfolded. Pleasure was banked from each new person I met. Magic always happened. I was lured to the stranger corners of the festival that consistently blew my mind. The perfect antidote to the rule book. Turn on, tune in, drop out—again.

I met an ex-soldier who'd recently left the Parachute Regiment and Helmand. He had shoulder-length black hair and wore a battered baseball cap and huge mirrored aviators. He nailed the white-trash trucker look, constantly grinning. Aged twenty-two, he'd survived the war and everything the army had to throw at him, and now his whole life was ahead to enjoy. He carted around a bottle of nitrous oxide and was knocking out balloons full of laughing gas—at a quid a pop. Teenage girls competed for his attention and queued for the balloons, and he loved every minute. We bonded over how awful Helmand was in comparison. Despite the professional rivalry between the Parachute Regiment and the marines, right there and then he was my brother.

Later that night we watched U2. I'd been a fan as a kid, seeing them at gigs a couple of times in my teens, but then I drifted away as they grew into their stadium phase. At the festival I was dragged along to see them by friends, and I'd rocked up belligerently, convinced there was nothing to enjoy. It was raining. They kicked off their set with Bono belting out the lyrics to their anthem "One": "We get to carry each other." Within two minutes my head was bowed, and I was shedding tears. Pathetic. For Christ's sake, I didn't even like this band anymore—get a grip. I was secretly relieved that the rain provided camouflage for my tears.

Over the next two nights I steadily progressed toward a state of mental obliteration, past caring about maintaining some semblance of dignity. I tripped over people, ending up on my back, laughing. Roger, my festival wingman and silverback gorilla, grabbed me by the scruff of the neck at the end of the night, marching us onward to the next episode of Shangri-La insanity. After the rigors of the desert, this was the best place in the world, the best medicine.

After the festival, for the next eight days, I didn't move from the cozy proximity of my family. Summertime glowed, and all I needed was to sit on the garden swing with the children and bury my face in their hair, breathing their smell. Life is poignant when you're on R&R and about to go back into the fray. The cool English climate did its best to lift me, but tendrils of melancholy wove tighter. I smelled the flowers as I ambled around the garden in the sunshine. Matt, a walking pin-pulled grenade and the toughest guy in our multiple, said that on the last day of his R&R during his first tour, he had wept with his parents in his back garden. His first tour, aged nineteen, had been hard—lots of casualties. On that R&R he was convinced he was going back to Helmand to die.

My daughter cried as I left. After I'd hugged everyone for the last time, I marched up the drive and jumped in the car without even glancing back, knowing they were looking at me and waving. I didn't want them to see me with tears in my eyes.

The departure lounge at Royal Air Force Brize Norton was full of troops heading back from R&R. There were at least 150 of us, but this time no one was smiling.

At Camp Bastion we had four hours' sleep before the 7 a.m. chopper flight back to our patrol base. Within twenty-four hours of leaving the UK, I was back at Zamrod getting rigged for a patrol. The efficiency was devastating. I couldn't believe it.

Everything was running like clockwork, except me. Something felt wrong. As I pulled on my boots, the backs of my thighs began to cramp up. Not just ordinary cramps, but huge evil spasms. Within moments I was writhing on the floor in agony, legs locking up in shapes impossible to break free from. Yoda saw me writhing, and within thirty seconds was on my case, ordering that I sit out this patrol and take some time to recover. I fought to regain control of my legs and resist the pain, saying I'd be OK. But Yoda wouldn't be swayed and insisted I stand down. I had mixed feelings: I was relieved not to be out on patrol at less than 100 percent but also felt bad because one of the other guys would have to take my place, pulling extra duty while I was just back from R&R, apparently the freshest man in the unit.

Any illness or minor injury incidents quickly became a source for complaining. Nearly everyone in 43 Bravo had spent time out of the game in the D&V (diarrhea and vomiting) isolation tent. But if anyone spent more than a day in there, it always caused resentment. Some of the men had been so ill they had spent three days there, but it brokered little sympathy from anyone. A man might be down, but the show still had to go on—patrols were never, ever canceled. Someone else who was able bodied would have to just step up and work harder. No one liked picking up the extra slack.

The cramps became completely debilitating, moving from my thighs to my entire legs, and concern grew about the creeping pain. I tried to figure out what had brought them on so quickly, and it didn't take long to figure out that all I had had to drink in the last thirty-six hours were a couple of glasses of water. Fine in the UK but completely inadequate hydration, bordering on hazardous, here in 120°F summer heat. You need six liters a day to operate in Afghanistan, and the official advice was to consume seven. I'd drunk less than one liter in the last twenty-four hours. I hadn't expected to be chosen to patrol so quickly, and this was a nasty wake-up call. I was back—but not in great shape.

The cramps lessened in severity but lingered. A twitch of a calf and the whole leg would snap into a painful spasm, forcing me to thrash and buck like an electrocution victim. Within eighteen hours I was back out on patrol—and it was one of the worst.

Yoda had committed to HQ that our patrol would be at a set location at a specific time. The destination was a couple of kilometers away, and we had to speed-march to make it to the rendezvous point on time. The pace was horrendous. Basic-training-test bad. Matt, the fittest of any of us, was on point, and as ever seemed to be the case, he carried the lightest load. I carried the ECM Red—a great lump of iron in a backpack with technologically sophisticated innards. Plus, the huge brick-sized spare batteries needed hauling, too. I soon was exhausted, the lingering dehydration making me feel ill.

Enemy gunfire erupted. Yoda was on the radio and told us that another team was engaged in a heavy firefight, and we had to yomp in double-quick time in support. Firefights broke out in several locations. Bursts of automatic weapons were coming from all directions. We tried to respond by cutting off possible Taliban escape routes, but there were too many areas in play, and we seemed to double back on ourselves again and again. After four hours of hunting, the decision was made to patrol back to Zamrod.

By this time it was pitch black, and the battery on the ECM unit needed changing. I fumbled in the darkness to change it and was monumentally pissed off to discover that the replacement didn't work either. Something had shorted out on the machine. I knew, irrefutably, that before we'd left I'd double-checked that the spare was charged. One of the other lads witnessed that it was charged too, so my arse was covered as far as that little integrity check was concerned. But the real problem was that for the remainder of the patrol, we had no electronic countermeasures cover for the spectrum provided by that ECM. Translated: we were exposed to all radio-controlled bombs between here and Zamrod.

Stress ballooned into an unwelcome dread as I fumbled in the dark with the dud battery. I felt responsible for exposing the men, even though the failure was a tech glitch. Sometimes these units just go tits up and stop working.

Yoda spoke. "OK, listen up! We have two choices: we can either yomp back to Zamrod without full ECM cover or stay out here in the boondocks with the Taliban all night and get the guys from Zamrod to resupply us with a fresh battery in the morning."

Overwhelmingly, the men voted to take the risk and head back to the fort.

As we patrolled back, my thighs began to seize up. Like a curse, the cramps crept back. I couldn't believe it. I'd drunk gallons of water and electrolytes in the last eighteen hours, yet they were back with a vengeance. Suck it up and move. As we snaked through the fields in the darkness, I noticed that the gap was growing dangerously wide between me and the man in front. His ghostly silhouette became increasingly difficult to make out in the darkness. Serious dread set in: it was looking like my lack of mobility would split the patrol up—an utter no-no. Jason, seeing me struggle, offered to take the ECM backpack. Although I'd been carrying it for six or seven hours now and my legs were in trouble, I declined.

"There's no shame in it, Al," he said.

But to me there was. I'd never given up on any patrol, ever. But the prospect of my legs seizing up completely and keeping the patrol out all night, with no prospect of resupply until the morning, was too awful to contemplate. The men would hate me for days. Half an hour later, things were so bad that another lad, Chris, actually did relieve me of the ECM, trading it for his own lighter backpack and a metal detector. Walking became immediately easier. As we crossed irrigated fields and muddy ruts, the cramps stayed away. I couldn't believe the difference in weight between the two backpacks! I felt like skipping and was elated that we'd all make it back tonight and, provided we didn't step on any booby traps, all in one piece.

Still, I felt ashamed. For the first time in my life, I'd had to be relieved of a piece of kit. The gratitude I felt for Chris was immeasurable. During the last nine months, in which we had worked together every day, he was the only marine that I hadn't really bonded with, even when I'd tried to start a conversation. Eventually, I'd reached the conclusion that he was either shy or didn't like me. Regardless, he showed his true colors in my hour of need and saved my bacon in hostile Nad Ali that night.

We made it back, but I suspected Matt wasn't pleased. He was one of several who had joined M Company from Recce Troop and was always the most vocal about maintaining high standards. He'd had his appraisal and was officially, based upon our evaluation system, "number-one marine" in M Company in terms of aptitude and performance. He was the senior marine in wartime experience, and with the skills he had developed in Recce Troop, I figured that, out of all the guys, he needed to be appeased. He had a prickly side; he was incendiary, always opinionated. But you couldn't fault his soldiering skills, exactly the kind of man you wanted by your side in a crisis. I approached him the next morning when we had the opportunity to have a quiet moment.

"Sorry about last night."

No response, obviously waiting for me to continue.

"I've come back from R&R and got these cramps because I hadn't hydrated properly on the way back out here from the UK. But I've turned it around and am necking stupid amounts of water to get it fixed. I'll be back in the game tomorrow."

His ego was not insignificant. Previously, we'd joked that in another life he would have been fronting a rock band. Now, he acknowledged my deference to his alpha status.

"Don't worry, Bud," he said. "Just don't let it happen again."

I took a moment to appraise the exchange. Hilarious. I'd just been professionally chastised by a guy young enough to be my son. What the fuck? But he was right. Lapses in standards would get us killed.

Privately, I was still mortified and brooded while in the sangar that night. I was pleased that Jason came up to relieve me at 2 a.m. He was my confidante. He had a six-year-old son living with his ex-wife. Two days previously while cleaning the galley, I'd overheard him on the satellite phone.

"Hi ya, Son. How you doin'? What you been up to then, eh? Really? Sounds fun—he must be a good mate if you can play together for that long. What else have you been doing? Cool. Listen, I'm sorry I missed your birthday but I'm kinda stuck out here. Has Mummy let you watch the DVDs I sent you as presents? Callum? Callum? Can you hear me? . . . Bollocks, fucking line's dead!"

He barely restrained himself from smashing the phone on the side of the galley table as he cussed under his breath. "Fucking piece of shit phone! Fuck it. Fuck everything."

And right now I was turning to him for help, saying, "I'm kicking myself about what happened on the patrol last night. Seriously, I'm thinking about wrapping, telling the sarn't major it would make sense if he found me another role. Honestly, for the first time last night, I actually felt like a fucking liability. I might be too old for this shit. Last night was a warning I should take a step back. This is a young man's game, and I don't want put anyone's life at risk again."

His response was robust. "Do me a favor and stop dripping! Don't be a pussy. You're a fucking marine! Get a grip and sort your life out, Royal. You didn't get here by accident. You got through training didn't you? This ain't no harder. Get over yourself, man the fuck up. Realize it's just a blip and get back in the game. Lighten up, mate."

He smiled kindly, looking right at me, eyes twinkling. This bloke from the rough side of the tracks wore his heart on his sleeve. My heart nearly burst in appreciation. In less than a minute, he'd turned me around from whining misery into having a fighting hope. He'd given me my confidence back—priceless. There was only one way out of the gloom and that was to get back on the horse. I vowed that if he ever needed me back home, I would drop everything for him. His best mate in the world had recently been blown up and killed for Christ's sake, and here he was, a sage, mopping up my insecurity, trying to make *me* feel good. The man was a fucking rock.

Out here, marines simultaneously filled the roles of friends, family, and colleagues. As an organization the corps was intensely social. We were always in extremely close physical proximity. Yoda was boss, yet he patrolled and ate meals with us every day. He slept every night in our tent, in a camp bed less than six feet away from me. One of us. This was an extraordinarily sociable place to work.

The company commander took half of 43 Bravo on a forty-eight-hour tasking, the last leg of which was a fourteen-hour patrol. The remaining eight of us stayed behind to man the fort, working three hours on, three hours off, for forty-eight hours. Monotonous and tiring in the extreme. We stopped complaining when we saw the condition of the men in the patrol when they returned. Several of them were howling crazily, like victims undergoing medieval torture, as they staggered back in through the main gate. "Arrgghh!" No real words. So exhausted that this was the only protest they could make. Coping with the sun and dust, humping kit the equivalent in weight of carrying a twelve-year-old kid, being hypervigilant for snipers and IEDs, needing to watch *every single step* they made—for fourteen hours. Enough to make you go crazy.

Patrols had taken a toll on all of us. By now half of us had open sores the size of a fist on both of our hips. They were webbing burns, caused when the body armor side plates rubbed the skin off our hips, right through our clothes. This was an age-old problem for bootnecks when they yomped and speed-marched for long distances. The men were resigned to it, applied Sudocrem, and soldiered on.

One day I was in the communal shower grappling with my two-liter bag of water (you really can shower with just two liters) when I grumbled to Jason that I couldn't understand why soldiering never seemed to get any easier, despite the advances in technology. He considered my comment for a moment and then replied that soldiering has not gotten any easier through the ages, and probably never will, because ultimately it's all about men hunting men. As one side innovates, the enemy adapts and catches up. And so it goes in endless circles of competition to survive. The technological advancements increased the odds of winning, not in making life easier for the fighting men. Life is hard for the frontline soldier and always will be, as long as other men were the quarry.

10

RULE NUMBER 2

Don't Shoot Civilians

Back in the patrol rotation, five minutes prior to setting out, there was a long, anguished scream. Pitiful, torturous—the bellow of a mortally wounded beast. It was Matt waiting by the gate, fully rigged for patrol. Before the gates opened we formed up and checked readiness: comms working, magazines firmly on, weapons ready and cocked (a round up the spout, safety catch on). The patrol commander sorted out the order of march, and the gate bitch for the day stood by to open the gate so we could make a quick exit. Standing near the gate, Matt was still wailing, other blokes were laughing, and the source of his pain was obvious. He was a seething bundle of testosterone—he must have more than a normal man's allocation. Sweat poured, his bandanna was soaked, and he hadn't even taken a single step out the gate. The temperature was about 125°F, and he was slowly cooking, constrained by the body armor and aware that within the next minute he was going to be humping it outside the wire. His frustrated howls were nothing more than a protest that he was *still* here—and he had only two choices: either go out that gate and face the long slog in the desert sun, risking injury and death, or face military prison for the crime of "refusing to soldier." He trudged through the gate, and the wails ceased.

The next task was the kind that most of us relished—a search mission in a suspected Taliban bomb-making factory. These missions were fascinating, and lives depended on us doing it properly. The suspect uninhabited compound was less than five hundred meters from Zamrod. We were hypervigilant and supercautious because we were in exactly the same scenario as JJ and his team had been when they'd been taken out by an explosive booby trap. Three men had been killed by that bomb.

It didn't take long to find detonators and other IED components, as well as a diary containing the names of Taliban commanders. All the evidence was tagged and bagged. Just as ominous were the hypodermic syringes that littered the floor in the rooms. I almost knelt on one as I bent down to give Yoda an update. Before long, men were finding used syringes strewn everywhere. Such a wicked place. The implications were stark: our base and home was five hundred meters from a nest of fundamentalists, hell-bent on martyrdom and smacked out of their heads, mainlining heroin.

In July, the villagers reported that they suspected an IED had been planted ninety meters from the fort in the tree line to our west. We patrolled out, skirting around the device before closing in to within twenty meters of it. We could see it buried right along the tree line. Jack, who, at nineteen, was the youngest of us, cautiously approached with the metal detector, clearly marking out the safe lane for the bomb-disposal guys.

We then found out that the underresourced bomb disposal team were preoccupied with higher priority devices, so they wouldn't be able to deal with ours. They took four days to show up. In the interim we cordoned off the site, patrolled (tiptoed) around it, and watched over from the sangar as it sat there, pregnant with menace. The digital rangefinder permanently ensconced in the sangar tower steadfastly refused to waiver in accuracy. Every time I picked it up, it precisely measured ninety meters to potential doom. The bomb-disposal team finally arrived and disabled it—in and out in forty-five minutes flat. Another pressure-plate IED neutralized. Thank you, gentlemen—we owe you. Again.

Still blistering hot we yomped up to the Nor Mohammed check-point. One of the marines from Recce Troop was struggling. "Think I'm goin' down," he mumbled. His face was crimson. Time to cool off. Arriving at Nor Mohammed we stripped off our body armor and waded fully clothed into the stream that ran through the base. We had less than five minutes of immersion—it was only about two feet deep—before we had to get our kit back on and get patrolling. It was sheer ecstasy floating on my back in the stream. Indescribable pleasure. Other submerged bootnecks were laughing in delight and relief. I couldn't believe how lucky the men were who were based here. They got this pleasure after every patrol.

We got back to the fort at 10 p.m., and I was up again at 4 a.m. to rendezvous with my friend, the sangar. At 5:30 a.m. we were off on another four-hour patrol. When I got back my shoulders were killing me. Dashim gave me a deep shoulder massage while I sat on a bench in the welfare tent. It felt like heaven—the first kind touch from another human in months. I told him it was the best thing to happen to me since I had gotten to Afghanistan—well, at least equal to that dip in the stream. He smiled, announcing proudly, "My grandmother taught me."

There were other moments of respite. Local friendlies began making daily deliveries of an eighteen-inch block of ice. At last, before the ice block melted, we could count on something cold to drink every day, just between 11 a.m. and 3 p.m.—by which time there would be nothing left of the ice except a bucket of warm water.

We took a delivery of powdered eggs. It was like taking another step back in time. The last time I had heard of *anyone* consuming that kind of food was in the Second World War. We were surprised it still existed. But we were all sick of the boil-in-the-bag menus and so couldn't wait to tuck in. Taff, a former chef, showed us how to cook a powdered-egg omelet.

Not too bad when seasoned with garlic salt, dried onions, and Spam. Delivered straight from the 1940s—a real treat. Things were looking up.

But I lost one of my key diversions, reading, when my Amazon Kindle broke due to the heat. I lost access to all my ebooks. Fuck it. This was the second Kindle that had broken in the last few months. They were way too fragile for this environment.

Other diversions were not so benign. On July 30 we heard a massive firefight erupt in J Company's area. They suffered one casualty. Some of the lads were selected to go out on a heli-borne op, so we had to man the fort with a skeleton crew again. Three hours on, three hours off, for the forty-eight hours of their mission. If insurgents had taken a crack at overrunning the fort in sufficiently high numbers, it wouldn't have taken much of a sustained effort to kill us all. It wouldn't be the first time that British troops had been overrun in a hostile outpost in a remote part of the old Empire. For the first time since we'd arrived, I felt vulnerable within the confines of the fort, even though we had the grenade machine gun, the general-purpose machine gun, various semiautomatic weapons, shotguns (affectionately christened "the zombie killers"), plenty of pistols, and grenades—basically enough to put up a decent fight and probably thwart a direct attack. That's what I kept telling myself at the time . . .

Two days later we linked up with the Afghan police who were helping to man a fort about a mile from us. We were sharing a cigarette and a bit of banter with some of them when one told me that he had four wives. Four! Imagine the hassle. Working with the police later that day, Chris discovered thirty-five kilograms of opium in one of the compounds we searched. It had been processed into a resin. How much heroin would that make? The Afghan army found the man hiding the opium, and they slapped him around the head and face in front of his hysterical wife and children. He was sent off for interrogation, with most of his family trailing after him, crying. He wailed, proclaiming his innocence, trying to convince the Afghan soldiers that the Taliban had forced him to hide it. One thing for sure, he was dirt poor, dressed in rags, trying to eke out a living. Chris was totally nonchalant about the opium find. This kid was just too cool for school, but I was pleased for us all, a rare occasion when we actually got a tangible result from a mission.

Patrolling three-quarters of a mile from the fort, a series of huge explosions erupted close by—*Jee-zus!* I jumped out of my skin, my heart slamming in my chest. The shock was so great that in the two seconds it took to come to my senses, I thought I was already halfway through a heart attack. You *felt* the power thunder through the ground and air. I was eager to find out what happened, but when I got back and started to de-rig, I noticed I'd been bitten on the wrist by an insect and it was swelling up nastily. Within fifteen minutes I was clobbered by sickness and nausea, and in another fifteen minutes I collapsed and started vomiting. Two of the guys picked me up off the deck; each hooked one of my arms over their shoulders and they walked—dragged—me to the medical point in one of the fort's ISO freight containers. Once there the vomiting started again. When it stopped they got me to a stretcher and hooked me up to an IV drip.

I was disoriented and couldn't stand the heat inside the ISO container, which was made of steel and had no windows—a perfect oven for the midday heat. I fought back the nausea and dizziness, grabbed the drip and the stretcher, and staggered out to find a piece of shade. I felt like an animal crawling off somewhere to die quietly. I found a sliver of shade less than three feet wide where the ops room ISO cast a shadow and lay there out of the sun's glare. I spent the next twelve hours there unable to do anything except groan quietly. Those were the worst hours of my life. I didn't expect any sympathy and didn't get any. We all knew that until I recovered, others would have to pick up the slack.

While I was recovering, a villager, age about thirty, came to the fort to see our medic, complaining he was in pain. He lifted up his dishdash, an ankle-length robe, and pulled down his trousers. His legs were heavily scarred, nasty looking. He told us his house had been destroyed by bombs from fast jets and he had been burned. He had been trying to live with the constant pain from the badly healed burns and was literally begging for something to relieve it. The nearest hospital was twenty miles away—a very long walk—so he had turned to us. The best our medic could do was give him some ibuprofen and Sudocrem, the stuff we ordinarily use for crotch rot and webbing burns, and send him on his way. Headache pills and nappy rash cream. Pathetic. He trudged away despondently. We felt like shit.

We had made a makeshift gym, and most men worked out there between patrols. Matt's physique stood out. He paced around the fort like a caged animal, his face and arms jutting skyward, blood vessels about to burst in his eyeballs, shouting to everyone and no one in particular, "For the love of fucking *God*, will somebody *please* just get me on the cover of *Men's Health* magazine! Just get me on the fucking cover—now!"

He was serious—in peak condition, ripped, lean—and looked formidable. A savage. A sleeve of tattoos covered an arm from shoulder to wrist. He'd have eaten the male-model cover stars of *Men's Health* for breakfast. No one complained about his exuberance. Just being around a warrior with such massive confidence was reassuring.

Laughs kept us going. If one of the men crept forward on their belly on a dirt track to confirm an IED, the young guys would sing the words to "I'm a Barbie Girl." They knew the whole song word for word. "I'm a Barbie girl, in a Barbie world, life in plastic, it's fantastic."

It was easy to conceive that they had come out of their mother's wombs invisibly tattooed with the motto "It's a grave mistake to take yourself too seriously." A failure of humor in a tight spot was a failure of character, and they knew this deep down in their DNA. High spirits kept everybody from going insane.

In the first week of August, another company got hit in a drive-by grenade attack at one of their checkpoints. A young marine, James Wright, was killed. Rest in peace, James.

I found out about the attack while on sangar duty listening to the BBC World Service on one of the windup transistor radios that we gave away to the locals. The somber archetypal voice of the BBC World Service radio presenter announced, "Today another Royal Marine has been killed in the Nad Ali district of Helmand in a grenade attack on a checkpoint." It startled me because I was hearing it first live on a global radio station. I became much more alert as it dawned that *I* was also in a checkpoint in Nad Ali. God bless the BBC, now I was *really* paranoid—the attack that had claimed James's life could be the first of a series on other checkpoints. At that very moment I heard gravel crunching below the sangar, toward the outer wall of the fort. My heart raced as I looked down from the tower, searching for the killers—two local dogs scavenging for scraps.

Ordinarily, when you're within the confines of the sangar, you tend to feel safe because of the four relatively high walls that surround you. However, all it takes for carnage to ensue is one insurgent cycling past and lobbing a couple of grenades over the wall. That is exactly what had happened at J Company just a day or so before and had killed James.

On August 8 we were sent to patrol into a town nearby to provide security for a military stabilization team (MST). Their role is to liaise closely with the Afghan civilians, running cash-for-works programs for small infrastructure projects, such as providing hygienic outside toilets for schools or clean water wells for villages. Tosh was a twenty-year-old sharpshooter from Liverpool; he had a habit of chewing a toothpick whenever we were out on patrols. That day, Tosh and I were working as bodyguards for an MST officer in a compound at a cash-for-works project site. The locals were building a tiny outhouse for a school, but the progress that had been made in the last couple of months was pitiful. Approximately thirty-five cinder blocks had been roughly built into a couple of shaky-looking walls. The MST officer looked exasperated at the lack of progress. He told us that this was typical: most often a portion of the money for a project was given up front, and so the locals were in no hurry to complete the construction.

While we were examining the work—or lack of it—a truly ungodly burst of gunfire erupted close to the walls of the compound. Tosh shot me a wide-eyed "holy shit" glance, but in the space of two seconds we realized there was no threat to life within the walls of the compound and so no need to take cover. Apache gunships were on the scene— their guns opening up in a roar, no doubt finishing the job. But what fascinated me was that while all hell was breaking loose a short distance away, the locals we were talking to never once paused in their activity. They were utterly unfazed by gunfire and explosions. They hadn't flinched or even batted the proverbial eyelid. In London people would be screaming and taking cover. As the firefight raged, they simply kept negotiating better terms for their project, trying to weasel more cash from the MST officer and more time to complete the outhouse. I marveled at how inured they had become. We were in a land that had endured armed conflict for more than thirty consecutive years, and for many of these people, war was all they had ever known.

Days later our company came under attack again: the marines from Fort Zulfakar were being engaged, and we yomped up to support them. It's a strange rush running toward a firefight, instinct telling you to move fast in the opposite direction from the battle. Exciting. My God, you feel so alive—such an almighty buzz! We had a new Afghan terp with us, whom we called John because no one could pronounce his real name. He was carrying the radio that transmitted Taliban radio chatter out of a small speaker, and today there was lots of it. Having access to their transmissions as they coordinated their attacks was invaluable, especially as they believed that their transmissions were private. This was a huge tactical advantage. We'd been out on hundreds of patrols with Dashim, but this was John's first, and we were all are wondering if he would hold up under the pressure and deliver—his literal trial by fire. He passed me a fluent real-time update of the insurgent chatter. I'd get the information and pass it up the chain of command. I was riveted listening to the Taliban voices as John translated, reporting that "Now they've seen us, and they've just described how we moved into this tree line!"

While we sat in that very same—now very deadly—tree line, John's radio aerial flopped about uselessly, and he had to maneuver it into position to hear a clear transmission. When he did this, it worked beautifully, the Taliban sounding less than twenty feet away. But then he'd gotten distracted and had let the aerial flop for a moment. I barked at him, jabbing a finger, "Fucking take charge of that aerial!" No need to flap—he'd already bent it into position, and the reception was so clear now you could hear the enemy panting between babbled Pashtun orders.

A transmission minutes later told us they were moving an IED into position now that we were getting closer. *Fuck me, this was electrifying!* Fascinating, critical, life-saving intelligence. You're listening to the live broadcasts of men who can see you *and* are trying to kill you, a battle of wits, more riveting than any entertainment ever created in the history of mankind. As the messages were quickly passed down through the team, our motivation skyrocketed—kill them before they kill us.

We found cover in the tree line and took up alternate firing positions. I faced east, spotting a youth on a rooftop looking in our direction—a dicker, the Taliban scout who alerts his comrades to our shifting positions so that they can attack. The rules of engagement stated that dickers could be shot on sight once they were positively identified. Unbeknown to the kid on the roof, his face was the target in at least four sets of telescopic sights in our patrol. Lee, our patrol commander, couldn't verify that the suspected dicker had a transmitting device. He might just be a teenager overcome with curiosity about the drama unfolding in his own backyard. The decision was made to spare him, since he couldn't be postively identified. He'll never know how close he came to meeting Allah that day.

With our way cleared we set off again toward the gunfire, letting the other call sign know that we were nearly at their location. But soon shooting erupted again in our direction, and we opened fire. We all felt the frustration of engaging an enemy who was a warrior one minute and a civilian the next. The insurgents thinned out and blended back in with the local population. As soon as the shooting stopped, someone reported another IED find, so we were tasked with yomping back to the company HQ to escort the bomb-disposal team back to disable it.

Two hours later we were still out on patrol, and another firefight erupted. Wilf, our platoon weapons instructor, caught a glimpse of a man half crawling through a field toward us. He aimed, fired, and the insurgent's head erupted in a red mist. Wilf got on the radio and reported in his inimitable, supernonchalant manner, "Er, I think we have another situation here . . ."

As we marched back to the Khammar HQ, kicking up clouds of dust at the end of that patrol, weariness was dragging me down. We only had five hundred meters left to go, but I had to dig deep to make it. I knew the other guys were as exhausted as I was. Our CamelBaks had run out of water hours earlier, and we had to resort to using the lifesavers—flasks that purified water scooped from irrigation ditches. After ten hours on the ground, a large part of it in a totally psyched and hyped state, I felt done in. I staggered inside the main gate, utterly spent. Thank God we had a thirty-minute break before we needed to patrol back home to Zamrod.

During the break the company sergeant major bought everyone a slush puppy from a machine shipped in the week before. Not a usual gesture for him, but one we all appreciated. Wilf was sitting next to me. A consummate professional career marine, this was his second tour in Helmand. Now, as he sipped his slush puppy, he reflected on how he'd deal with the officers who would be conducting the investigation of his kill.

"You worried?" asked Lee.

"Nah. I'll tell 'em the truth. My priority was the safety of the men."

The investigation was quickly closed. It was that easy.

The morale of the marines on that patrol was soaring. You could feel the buzz. For many of the younger men, it had been their first enemy contact, and they relished the combat. Elation was written all over their faces, their banter funnier, louder, more merciless. We'd taken on board all the evil shit that Helmand could throw—heat, weight, firefights, bombs—and, in the colloquial parlance of the young men I worked with, we'd smashed it.

As evening set in we prepared to leave Khammar. The sergeant major caught my eye, greeted me, then frowned, squinting closely. "Jesus Christ, Seymour!" he said, grimacing. "You actually look worse than a fucking AIDS victim!"

He'd quipped previously that it looked like I'd had a hard paper route as a boy, one that started when Columbus was discovering America. Now, for the first time ever, momentarily, he looked like he was actually slightly concerned. But no, he just turned and marched back into the ops room to address more pressing matters. This was his third year here. I remember what he had said back during training at Camp Bastion, when we'd shared a cigarette during a lull in training (we didn't smoke in the UK, but here cigarettes sustained us). He'd taken a drag and exhaled, shaking his head. "Thirty-six months of my life spent in this shithole . . ." A rueful silence followed. During that moment we both knew that our ranks and uniforms were just roles we were playing—transient, impermanent. The camaraderie in that moment had nothing to do with our environment: it was all about our age, twice as old as most of the others. My admiration ran deep. I struggled to think of him as anything other than being an inspiration—he had the secret sauce. He galvanized us, relentlessly slaving night and day for the men under his command. He knew his job inside out and was often at his gut-busting funniest when taking the piss out of some hapless marine. I secretly wished for him that this tour, his final, passed quickly and safely.

The sun was setting as we hobbled back into Zamrod. While unloading our weapons, Matt remarked, "You did well today, mate. Strong."

I muttered some kind of acknowledgment, but inside my heart was soaring. That was the first chuck up (compliment) Matt had given me since the dehydration problem patrol more than a month ago. I knew we'd all put in a good effort that day, and it had been noted. Matt, the lucky bastard, had been riding the quad bike for much of the day, accompanying us on our route, and he'd seen how much the lads had to dig out. A quintessentially gruff Yorkshireman, he didn't make a habit of complimenting people, so I knew he was being sincere. Everything was now OK in my world. Ordinarily, back in the UK, I wouldn't have cared, but out here it was different. These men—every single one of them—never, ever capitulated. Never—not out here. They knew they were undergoing the test of their lives, and they gave it their all and would march and fight on until they dropped. Even if injured, they'd be concerned for the welfare of the other men in the patrol—a force for good.

We heated up some beef stew, ate, and slept. But were awakened in the middle of the night to get back up for sangar duty, and then we were up for good at 6 a.m. and back out on patrol at 7 a.m.

Later that day I saw Tosh and his team arriving from a twelve-hour patrol. I'd missed that one due to the luck of the draw. As he got de-rigged, I asked what it had been like. I knew full well, but wanted to hear this twenty-year-old kid describe it. He looked me dead in the eye, wiped his nose on his sleeve, his face practically pressed against mine, and as he ripped off his chest rig, he spat, "Disgusting!" His first complaint that I'd heard since we'd got here. He sniffed and asked, "Spare cigarette, mate?"

I passed him a Marlboro Light and sparked it up. We smoked in silence, and I thought about his mother. Not for the first time in my imagination I told her, I dearly hope that you're proud of your son. You should be. He's truly one of the good guys, an asset to mankind.

11

Farewell to Zamrod

The two wireless Internet–connected laptops in the welfare tent were off being repaired, so all I had left for entertainment were podcasts on my iPod. All the shared paperback books were falling apart—literally. No one had warned us that books would disintegrate in the heat. The glue in the binding that holds the pages to the spine just melts, and after only two reads, all the paperbacks strewn around the tent were little more than heaps of loose pages.

In other respects things were looking brighter. In mid-August we patrolled up to 42 Commando's HQ in Shazad, loading up on cigarettes and fizzy drinks on arrival. And, naturally, since we were at a fort that had them, we necked as much fresh food and cold drinks as we could. The chefs gave us a cooked lunch—the first one in four months, a real coup—of sweet-and-sour chicken. I also managed to get hold of a juicy pear. Fresh fruit! Then the sergeant major obliterated the downtime, crashing into the tent barking, "Seymour, get the team together now! A Mastiff's been hit by an IED on route Nike. We need to secure the area."

Before long the team was together, patrolling toward the blast area. The bomb had gone off five hundred meters south of Zamrod. The night before I had walked right over it on a patrol down to the next checkpoint at Shurin Junction. The ISAF forces had built a school there for the local Afghan children, and we had to maintain a presence in the area to stop the Taliban from blowing it up.

On another patrol the night before, Matt had protested saying that he didn't want to walk back to Zamrod the same way along route Nike. He had covered his face with his hands in a moment of resignation and a feeling of dread. "Seriously, lads, I've got a fucking bad feeling about this."

Taff agreed. "Yeah, I'm with you—I'd rather stick my face in a box of rattlesnakes."

Matt's intuition was overruled, and we were ordered to walk the route.

Because we'd already patrolled down route Nike the previous day, we realized we had all walked over the same unexploded bomb twice in twenty-four hours. It must have been extremely well hidden, as I'd scrutinized the entire route, and the other men had done exactly the same, watching every single step, suspicious of any unnatural ground sign. No one had seen a thing. We were lucky, and so were the marines in the Mastiff vehicle when it exploded. Despite the extensive damage to the vehicle, no one had been hurt. It takes a lot of explosive to destroy a seventeen-ton heavily armored wagon. Matt had been on the sangar at Zamrod, while most of us had been at Shazad, and he saw it detonate. The roof of the sangar nearly blew off, and the explosion lifted the Mastiff off the ground, ripping off a layer of armor, while the rest of the armor had done its job and saved the lives of the men.

At set times during the day, the village loudspeaker would put out the call to prayer that lasted for five minutes of singing. But every Friday at four o'clock in the morning—o'crack sparrow fart—the peace was shattered by the voice of the local mullah haranguing the villagers through that same loudspeaker. If you were dead tired, returning from a patrol or just off sangar duty hoping for a few precious of hours sleep at 4 a.m., you were in for an ungodly awakening and an apocalyptic sense of woe. Was there no avoiding these men? His rant lasted a whole bastard hour, an excruciatingly shrill string of venomous curses spat upon a hated enemy. Some of the ugliest human sounds I'd ever heard. Even if you didn't know the language, you could tell this was a vicious tirade. I asked Dashim what the hell the mullah was shouting about every Friday morning at 4 goddammed a.m., and he told me that he was chastizing the villagers for not being better Muslims. So one morning, still incredulous at the ferocity of the mullah's rant, I recorded the full, unabridged tirade on an iPod. I planned to bet friends at home ten pounds that they couldn't endure listening to it at the same volume we'd had to for more than ten minutes (imagine huge speakers pointed directly at your house and the volume turned to full). A tenner bet for ten minutes of grief—practically a done deal.

The heat—my nemesis—undid me again. Near the end of the tour, I went down with heat exhaustion on patrol. We had a new, highly capable naval medic called Ruth assigned to us, living in the patrol base and joining us on patrols. The local children always swarmed around her, wide-eyed and fascinated, giving her the full "unicorn" treatment; small hands reached up to touch the blonde hair beneath her helmet, confirming she was real. Now, ten minutes after the patrol, she took my resting pulse: 177 beats per minute. Not good. After previous difficulties with the heat, I knew that this incident would mean my time at Zamrod serving with 43 Bravo was over. As this was the second heat-related incident I had had in the last five months, I would have to undergo tests to determine if I now had a predilection toward heat-related injuries. I didn't have any say in the matter, as Yoda had already radioed the incident ahead. A Mastiff vehicle would be passing by, and he ordered me on it.

I had fifteen minutes to get my kit packed, say good-bye to everyone, and get on board that Mastiff for the journey up to the company HQ, where a doctor awaited. I hastily said my good-byes to the lads and packed up. The Mastiff arrived; I threw my gear on the roof and jumped in the back. All I could think of as Zamrod faded into the distance was that just the day before a new solar panel had been installed on our fridge. After nearly six months in this heat hellhole, I had managed to enjoy precisely one day of chilled water.

Afghan kids hurled rocks that clanged noisily off the side panels as we rumbled along through the dust. Imagine putting your head in a steel bucket and someone hitting the bucket with a hammer—same noise. In the space of fifteen minutes, I'd gone from being a member of the team in Zamrod to being ousted. I felt sad to be leaving the men. This was not the proper way to depart. I knew already that my days on the front line were over. As I rattled around the inside of the Mastiff, with no windows, no distracting views, I grew introspective and pondered my next big move.

On arrival at Bastion the doctor announced, "Congratulations on joining the three hundred club."

"Eh?"

"One hundred patrols in over 100°F heat, carrying one hundred pounds of kit. You're in."

"Fair enough, but I'll just take the campaign medal, thanks."

She told me two British servicemen had died from heat exhaustion, so doctors were paying attention to the problem. Anyone who showed susceptibility would be assigned a noncombatant role. Basically, I was about to become a REMF (rear-echelon motherfucker). Frontline soldiering always has been, and would continue to be, a young man's game. Time to call it a day.

Bastion provided significantly more comfort than Zamrod. I was finally able to get a full night's sleep—every night. The food was excellent. I looked around the galley and felt proud of the men and women in there. It was huge, catering for eight hundred people. Senior officers, navy medics, army counter-IED specialists, air force, soldiers, marines, doctors, special forces, engineers all mingled, laughing and chatting. The sense of shared purpose was palpable—an enormous team that required massive collaboration, people dedicating their best efforts to this cause. Looking around the galley I almost pitied the Taliban.

Physically, mentally, ideologically, they were no match for the people in this room. And, unlike the murky motives behind the recent war in Iraq, most of the people here believed, as I still did at this stage, that the cause in Afghanistan was just. This wasn't a conflict that you could "win" in the classic military sense. But people did what was needed to make the task force succeed—providing governance, infrastructure, and security while we were here.

Gandhi had said during the Indian struggle for independence from colonialism, "I do believe that, where there is only a choice between cowardice and violence, I would advise violence." We live in a complex world. Tyrants exist. Of course, you had to wonder what would happen when we left this war-torn country. The political motives for the coalition military presence here might be even murkier than those of Iraq. Who knows? Meanwhile, exit please.

I pitched up in the medical tent with the other marines there. Three of them had been injured by a grenade thrown into their compound. One of them still had shrapnel in him, so I used the pliers of my Leatherman tool to dig tiny pieces of the grenade from his feet. The doctors had managed to get most of it, but there was still plenty left to work on. All three marines were keen to return to their units and get back in the fight. I couldn't help but notice how different these young men were from the young men who had been rioting in Britain's streets the previous week. Those kids back home were causing mayhem for a pair of brand-name running shoes. Culturally, they came largely from the same social strata as many of these marines, but their values were a world apart.

Four marines from my original company—L Company—were injured in an IED blast. Two sustained Cat A (catastrophic) injuries, and two were Cat Cs. I thought of them as I listened to a podcast later that night and heard the phrase, "All I've got in this world is my balls and my brain, and I ain't breaking them for nobody."

I was happy to run into Yoda and Matt as they were returning from a five-day op with L Company. The worst five days of their lives. It had been even worse for the Taliban. Ten Taliban had been killed. Some of Bastion's most formidable weapons—rockets and laser-guided bombs—had done their job during the op and taken out the insurgents. One of the marines I spoke to said you could look into the target compound with aerial thermal-imaging cameras and see the warmth still rising from the dead bodies.

Our multiple had been luckier than most in that our time at Zamrod hadn't been as kinetic as it had for other multiples, such as those in L Company. I heard about more firefights when I bumped into another friend, TC, a marine reservist serving in L Company. We had spent time the previous summer training in the Sierra Nevada mountains. In his late twenties, TC hadn't been out of basic training very long but was already seasoned and extremely adept. With his wraparound antiballistic shades, green bandanna, and oversized unshaven jaw, he was like an American military caricature, straight out of central casting for the movie *Predator*. Back in the real world, he'd gone to university, spoke fluent Spanish, and was a pediatric nurse. This was one of the reasons he enjoyed taking on the Taliban. He cared about children's welfare and was professionally dedicated to it. The Taliban routinely blew up the schools that ISAF forces had built. Many marines saw these jihadist extremists as an existential threat and a threat to the development of humanity. Proof was Malala Yousafzai the girl (and now Nobel Prize winner) shot in the head for attending school. Unforgivable. As far as TC was concerned, that alone provided justification enough to hunt and kill them. Over the last few months, he'd been in countless battles, and he grinned widely as he told me how much he enjoyed it.

So far, 42 Commando had lost seven men killed in action and suffered eighty-three casualties. The longer I served with these men, the more I viewed marines as masters of pain management. Much as I loved the corps, that's how I viewed it—an institution that teaches you how to cope with pain. Despite all the bravado, most marines I talked to had had enough and just wanted to go home. I knew for sure that I was ready to leave. I was almost through my year-long reenlistment. As the tour came to an end, I wasn't going to figure out anything substantive about the moral questions about the war with my two bits' worth of musing. I hunkered down and worked through my final week with an entertaining six-foot-five sergeant major in the unit's command company. He had previously served a tour in Iraq leading a troop.

Each day I'd strip down the gear from the unit's battle casualties. A lot of it was covered with congealed and dried blood from catastrophic hemorrhage injuries caused by gunshots, grenades, and IEDs to marines' necks, heads, and limbs. I'd think about the man the kit belonged to as I stripped it down, itemized the contents, packed it all up in boxes, and shipped it back to the UK. Compared to the regime of nonstop patrols at Zamrod, this was the easiest job in the world.

During a break for lunch one day, I took the bus with some US Marines over to their PX store to get some American sweets for my kids.

"Where you from?" I asked the marine who was sat next to me.

"Paradise, California. It's a small town northeast of San Francisco. It's real nice."

I frowned and said, "So let me get this straight. You left your home in Paradise to come and fight in Helmand?"

"Yup," he said, with zero recognition of the irony.

One thing was certain about returning home: I wouldn't immediately go back to my old life. I needed a couple of months of contemplation. I'd had twenty years of beach holidays, but after six months in the desert, the last thing I needed was more sand, a beach bed, and a deeper tan. I craved more—something very special. I vowed to do everything I could to leave the darkness of Helmand behind. The insecurity I'd picked up as a youngster from my stepfather had been vanquished, and the validation I needed from serving during a war had been delivered.

I brooded as I stripped down those bloodied kit, boxing up dead men's belongings to be shipped home. There must be more to life. What now? What's next?

An idea began to take hold. Afghanistan was just the first stage of a much-needed quest. I was transforming from someone needing an adventure into a person seeking the truth about consciousness, spirituality—why we are here. During this time-out from civilian life, my inquiry had shifted from its gender-dominated expression— wondering about the nature of manhood. I was no longer interested in learning how to be a good man. What was of more interest was how to be good. And also how to become a person who could seize the value of every remnant of life.

Many of us believe that, despite their prevalence, traditional faith-based religions do not deliver any sort of sustaining satisfaction. Yet millions still yearn for spiritual fulfillment, while having no idea how to gain it. We grapple with the quandary that logic, rationality, and science practically *demand* the denial of spirit. Modern secular life is devoid of anything genuinely mystical or magical. But quite possibly there really is something present—a higher force to inspire and comfort. I knew for certain that the modern industrialized lifestyle and the prevailing paradigm of scientific rationality left no room for any divine element in my life. Whichever way I looked at it, there was a gap to fill, and for the first time in my life, I actually had the inclination and the time to explore it. I was still on a mission—but now a mission of a different kind. Breaking free of the military brotherhood and the experience of war would lead me to a new opportunity to see if it was possible to connect with the Maker and, critically, accomplish this *without* the aid of any existing faith-based religions. I had already seen enough of their failings, particularly those born out of the desert lands in the Middle East. These Abrahamic desert faiths had originated from a sense of scarcity, had sin and shame embedded at their very heart, and control was their ultimate agenda.

Based upon my earlier experiences with DMT and mushrooms, I had the unshakable conviction that there really was more to this life than meets the eye. The original plant source of the DMT was the lure; the Amazonian Natives called it ayahuasca. So, like a bee to pollen, the Amazon inexorably became a powerful attractor, drawing me to it.

I untethered the belief that masculinity should be tested and my life put at risk for a cause worth dying for. My first stepfather had inadvertently sparked my inquiry into the nature of manhood: what it means to be a good man and a good father. Since then I'd sought to learn how good men deliver stoic kindness and compassion in difficult circumstances—because he robbed me of the experience when it mattered, as a child. He forced me to seek out the company and character of good men. Since the birth of the Royal Marines in 1664, the marines poster that aimed to recruit "A Few Good Men" had been nailed to many a tavern's timbers, with no doubt the world's rustiest nails. What did "good" mean? What were the qualities? In the year working with Taff, Yoda, Matt, the sergeant major, the commanding officer—in fact, every single man in 43 Bravo, some of whom were barely old enough to be called men—I'd never witnessed a single brazen act of selfishness.

This particular inquiry into the nature of manhood had been sated. I had grown. Now I needed to go a step further. The drama we were surrounded by in this godforsaken place had to mean something. JJ had been taken out by trauma, and I hadn't. Why? Mere luck, or was it something to do with another role I had yet to play out? It was time to seek out a bigger question: How does a person become and feel enlightened? Why fuck about? *That* was the question. I still had an extensive period of postdeployment leave, and so I now had an opportunity to seek out the truth that was true for me. Furthermore, I was determined that this next step on the road to "wisdom" would have precisely nothing—*nothing*—to do with organized religion. There is a type of man out there—I'm one—who finds nothing in all the spiritual wisdom preached and written, who remains cynical. It's all meaningless yak, yak, yak, yak—until a natural psychedelic is consumed, and only then will the divine be *experienced* directly, not through a sermon. My friend David had already lit the psychedelic torch and helped me navigate with a rough mental map. I needed to learn and experience the nature of the Source for myself, by direct personal experience, not by listening to priests, sermons, or religious fables—all the frailties of fallible human beings projected onto false and nonexistent deities and megalomania-cal doom gods. I could never have done this in Afghanistan because my mind had been constantly preoccupied and locked into either two modes of consciousness—surviving or sleeping. There was no room or time for real contemplation.

Now, I felt I had two choices. The first was to go via the traditional route—northeast to the Himalayas or another Buddhist region—and seek enlightenment with a guru. But that approach didn't fit well; it had almost become a late twentieth-century cliché. The other choice was to go southwest to South America, commune with a shaman, and drink ayahuasca. There was never any question as to which option to take. Based on my experience with DMT, it was obvious that for me the Amazon was where the answers lay. It seemed to me that the Eastern philosophies and practices in the meditative Buddhist traditions are all about striving, reaching, seeking. With natural plant psychedelics the opposite is true—I'd already discovered it in the seven seconds after I'd smoked DMT with David. You don't have to strive or seek for anything! It's all instantly available to you—just consume the plant containing the psychedelic magic. Whether you "believe" or not is irrelevant. No mat-ter who you are, you *will* feel the power of the entheogen—like it or not. I knew already that spiritual experience isn't somewhere out there; it is right here, inside us. For me, the shaman in the jungle held the key. I decided the next step to delving deeper was to drink a very special kind of jungle juice in the Amazon.

During my last few days at Bastion, I searched the Internet for trips to South America. Research revealed that there were no known cases of anyone dying directly from the consumption of ayahuasca. For a healthy, psychologically well-adjusted person, the risk is minimal. Even though my previous experience with DMT had been relatively limited, it had shown its own power, which had induced a genuine sense of hum-bling awe. My consciousness had expanded in ways beyond description or comprehension. I felt unified with the cosmos and nature, attaining depths of feeling I would never forget. The experience had been so profound, fascinating, and beneficial that I couldn't wait to tell my children when they were old enough to properly understand. I wanted them to know that there is more to who and what we are than Western consumer culture leads us to believe. I made a simple list about why taking ayahuasca made sense:

1. It is 100 percent natural and organic, brewed up like a tea.
2. It is generally safe. Thousands of people have taken it over the centuries without deaths or injury.
3. An ex-Royal Marine officer called Bruce Parry had consumed it with Natives in the jungle and had a very positive experience. The BBC funded, filmed, and broadcast his experience to millions of British people.
4. It is known by indigenous people to have healing properties and provide spiritual nourishment and is renowned to be a "teacher" plant.
5. It is legal in the country where I'd be taking it.
6. It makes you feel *good*.
7. DMT, the active ingredient, occurs naturally and endogenously in the brain's neurochemistry.

To go through the rest of life without further inquiry into these mysteries would be a huge loss—like only using one-half of your brain. To deny the insights gained through exploring this option would be like having the Buddha, Jesus, Krishna, and Keith Richards turn up for dinner, recording the event on an HD camera, and then dismissing it as a mere daydream. With a small budget and an inquisitive mind, I could give myself this. So, as I packed up to head home from Afghanistan, I was already planning my foray into the Amazon. It was important to find a group that provided more than a tourist's romp through the jungle. I wanted to be guided by legitimate and responsible people. Looking online I stumbled across two appealing ayahuasca-related websites, both offering retreat-type ventures. One was called the La Kapok Center, and another was enchantingly named the Mythic Voyage. After Helmand, a Mythic Voyage was exactly what was needed. After scrutinizing many websites, I knew these two were for me.

My mission was transitioning into a once-in-a-lifetime, perhaps insane, inquiry into the *real* nature of life. A tall order. Men I knew and admired had been blown to pieces. I needed the real deal to make sense of the world, something epic. Little did I know at the time, one man had already conceived, organized, and delivered exactly what I was looking for. Even better, he was doing it all over again and would put me on his team and take me under his wing. I was about to embark on the wildest, craziest journey of my life—one that would match Afghanistan for freaky and unwelcome surprises and yet offer insight into the deepest human longings, which war could never deliver. All I had to do was lose myself in the jungle, relinquish control utterly, and trust that everything would turn out well.

La Kapok Center offered a stay deep in the Peruvian Amazon jungle where an American man, Richard, had built a retreat center and had a team of local Shipibo, including a master shaman, who led the ayahuasca ceremonies. Accommodation was basic, and they required that guests follow the strict diet necessary to prepare yourself to imbibe the psychotropic brew. As was customary, the ceremonies took place communally in a large circular lodge called a *maloca*. That's where I'd head first. Depending on how that went, I'd continue on to the Mythic Voyage.

With the plans in place, I flew back with the men I'd joined 42 Commando with to start the decompression period required before we could leave for home. Decompression is a mandatory forty-eight-hour stopover in sunny Cyprus, where activities included enforced "fun" in the guise of a four-hour beach visit, a strict rationing of beer and wine, and a live-entertainment show with a couple of singers and a comedian. It was a great show, and despite the fact that all of us just wanted to get home and see our families, the decompression time was welcome. Laughs rang around the auditorium as the comedian cracked his jokes. The music act was sufficiently rousing that soldiers in the front two rows were inspired to join them in belting out the lyrics of Florence and the Machine's "You've Got the Love" to each other. I'd enjoyed this song in one form or another during adult life but never imagined hearing troops singing it to each other with platonic love for their compatriots. The song had always been significant, and I'd enjoyed the Frankie Knuckles version all the way back to my early twenties. Now, as they sang the lyrics, these troops had their arms wrapped around their friends' shoulders and were looking into one another's eyes, singing their hearts out in a moment of shameless sentiment. They were serenading one another, and it was both hilarious and moving to witness. They had suffered and now it was over. The lump in my throat and hair that stood on end was a testament to the perfect fit of the song.

Sometimes it seems the going is just too rough
And things go wrong no matter what I do
Now and then it seems that life is just too much
But you've got the love I need to see me through

You've got the love, indeed. Underscoring all the revelry was a palpable sense of relief—we had made it out alive. Time to go home.

Arriving home was pure elation. Once the emotions of being home settled, integration back into family life was effortless. My first instinct was to spend as much time as possible being physically close to the children.

I felt so lucky to have found my wife, Julia. When I told her about my desire—my need—to go into the Amazon so soon after my return home, she agreed. She explained that seeing me come back alive was such a relief that a trip to the Amazon felt like far less to worry about. She knew I needed some downtime to decompress my way. She agreed that I could go, on the basis that I support her to move out of her career and retrain as a health and well-being practitioner. The qualifications she needed would take several years to acquire, and during this transition period, it would fall upon me to do the lion's share of the childcare. Homework supervision, cooking, kids' sports clubs—all mine to look forward to when I got home while she juggled motherhood, work, and study.

But I wasn't quite ready to head out to the Amazon yet. I had a few things to do first.

My mother volunteered to look after the children, and I took a holiday with Julia. We went to a sunny Mediterranean island for five days and danced. Each night fully immersed, surrounded by thousands of euphoric loved-up revelers, beautiful people, floating in Space, heaven-bent on having the best time of their lives. To top it all, a sublime remix of Florence and the Machine's "You've Got the Love" thundered through the speakers, the lyrics and melody an eargasm in a perfect setting that delivered everything I needed: life, wife, and music. Thank you, God. I don't know who you are—or what you are—but thank you, thank you, *thank* you . . .

Another priority was repatriation with JJ. He was at Headley Court, a veteran's hospital where they do amazing rehabilitation work. Nearly four months after his injury, he could walk unaided, but his right arm was still in rough shape. The only way he could move it was by manipulating it with his left hand, and that hand itself was missing several fingers. His face seemed vaguely different to me. I couldn't pinpoint why. Eventually he explained that he'd had extensive plastic surgery, with surgeons inserting a plate to reconstruct his smashed eye socket. Incredibly, they did this without leaving any trace of the surgery. The net result was a slight reshaping of his face that actually made him slightly better looking!

We jumped in my car and headed to a pub, where he filled me in on the details of the explosion that had injured him and three other men and had killed three more. The details were horrendous. Initially, after the blast, he'd been in so much pain that the nurses couldn't administer any more painkilling drugs without increasing the risk of death. Among those drugs were huge doses of ketamine. For a long time he'd become paranoid, believing that the nurses were trying to kill him. He interrupted his story for a moment to stand up, in the middle of the pub, and drop his trousers to show the damage to his legs. Massive blast scars covered his thighs, but at least they were still well muscled and working properly. He had several more operations to undergo. But hearing him talk, seeing his attitude, was such a relief. Despite everything that had happened to him, he was still exactly the same man.

We talked about what was next for each of us. He was going back to his teaching career—*after* he climbed Mount Kilimanjaro. The expedition was being funded by a veteran's charity, and JJ was on the team. Of course he was climbing Africa's highest mountain, I thought. Being JJ, what else was he going to do?

I explained about the pull of the brew called ayahuasca. Within a week I would be on a plane to the Amazon. I don't think he really understood, but he wished me well. I didn't know it at the time, but I would need those good wishes and more because deep in the cradle of the Amazon, things would get weird—weirder than I could possibly have imagined.

PART 2

THE MYTHIC VOYAGE

12

Power in the Jungle

Folks, it's time to evolve. That's why we're troubled. You
know why our institutions are failing us, the church,
the state, everything's failing? It's because, um—they're
no longer relevant! We're supposed to keep evolving.
Evolution did not end with us growing opposable thumbs.
You do know that, right? There's another 90 percent of
our brains that we have to illuminate.

BILL HICKS, COMEDIAN

Power accomplishes what force cannot do because it goes
where force cannot follow.

DAVID R. HAWKINS

My attention heightened as we flew over the Amazon, struck by the
incomprehensible enormity of the jungle. Iquitos is a gateway city to the
Peruvian Amazon, my first stop on the way to the La Kapok Center. I
spent two nights in Iquitos organizing the boat trip that would take me
four hours upriver to the small settlement of Herrera. While on that
journey, as the small boat motored upriver, I couldn't help marveling
at the contrast between Afghanistan and the Amazon—the difference

in the environments was staggering. The lush abundance of natural resources and the warm waters of the river contrasted sharply with the arid, hostile desert.

At Herrera I met Richard, the founder of La Kapok Center, and a Southeast Asian woman who had also contacted him for this ayahuasca adventure. Miley was in her midforties and had made the journey from Singapore. As we introduced ourselves and talked a bit, I learned she was married to a futures trader and had a fifteen-year-old daughter. She'd worked for Microsoft for many years and so was familiar with the company I worked for.

Richard was a friendly American and quintessentially clean-cut, with short dark hair and broad shoulders and a six-foot-two athletic build. He sported a Panama hat, and his white T-shirt and khaki cargo shorts were immaculate. Prior to settling in the Amazon, he had worked in finance on Wall Street. He had become disillusioned with the industry and turned his back on it. He had lived in Thailand for three years and was streetwise—dump him in the midst of twenty young marines, and he would thrive among the merciless piss taking. If you were to view Richard as the result of a social experiment in what happened to a "normal" person after years of committed ayahuasca use, then he could be the poster boy for an "Ayahuasca Needs You" ad campaign.

He explained about ayahuasca: to the indigenous people it is a sacred healing plant, which is why it is often referred to simply as *la medicina.* "It is *the* healing plant of the Amazon," he explained. "It heals me, you, society, spirit, our species. And love is the connection through which it heals. Love is the connection you really will understand."

Over lunch we continued to get to know each other. After we had paid Richard and his team for their services, he led Miley and me to the motorized canoe that would take us into the jungle.

Within half an hour we rounded a bend, tucked into a small tributary, and then came ashore at the retreat settlement that Richard had built from scratch. It comprised just a few buildings. Richard showed us around the kitchen, dining area, and bedrooms. There were about ten bedrooms in total, each a small hutlike room, one adjoining the other with only a six-foot-high rough-hewn wood partition/wall separating them. Each room contained a bed with a mattress and clean sheets. I dumped my large black North Face holdall in the corner of one room, taking all of ninety seconds to unpack.

We were then given a quick tour of the surroundings set in 250 acres of prime jungle habitat. Richard had found a location that dazzled, nestled in a gorge. The river that ran through it fluctuated between a wide and powerfully destructive torrent that uprooted trees and boulders to a relatively gentle stream no more than twelve feet wide that you could wade in when the water level was low. The location's crowning glory was a literally breathtakingly stunning waterfall, about thirty-two feet wide with a thirty-foot drop. The wide pool at its base spilled over another precipice to form a second waterfall of equal height. At the foot of the second waterfall was another large pool in which we could swim surrounded by hummingbirds and blue morpho butterflies the size of saucers. Even in the dry season, the waterfalls' thundering was loud enough to drown out voices. Thick vines drooped down from the canopy offering the temptation to reach out and grab one to see whether it could hold my weight. Huge slabs of flat rocks offered themselves generously as natural sunbathing platforms either side of the top pool, right at the waterfall's lip. The crash of the water drowned the sounds of the jungle birds and insects, and as I stared at and listened to the cascade, I was wrapped in a soothing, hypnotic feeling.

Richard told us that we were the only guests except for a young man who had been staying at the camp and would be joining us for ayahuasca sessions. His name was Reuben, aged nineteen, Norwegian, a recovering drug addict who had already been at the retreat center for three weeks, working on getting clean.

Richard surprised us by announcing that the first ayahuasca ceremony would happen that night. Prior to our arrival he had asked us to reflect on our intentions for the visit. We needed to set some personal goals as we voyaged with the shaman and the plant. Mine were simple: recover. After months of anxiety I needed to relearn how to be content. I was lucky not to have PTSD, and I wanted to use this time to reflect and send out good intentions for the families of the men in my unit who had lost their lives or limbs. Furthermore, following the war, I wanted to know how I could integrate back into society and be inspired. I had been wrestling with this concern. With all the intensity experienced over the last year, slotting back into previous roles might be challenging, and I was concerned I'd be hampered by the humdrum aspects of modern life.

The first ceremony began at 6:30 p.m. It gets dark quickly in the jungle with its thick canopy, and it was already twilight as we gathered in the *maloca,* a huge, wooden circular hut with a domed ceiling. It had a windowlike space in the wall covered with gauze that ran around the circumference of the entire room so that it was exposed to the outside except for a fine mesh to keep out the insects. All the ceremonies took place here. Hammocks hung low, their supports affixed to the ceiling, and rocking chairs made of wire and cord were positioned around the space, as were several mattresses. At the back of the room were several toilets that could be flushed using a bucket of water. The floors were bare wood, and the conical ceiling was impressively high and supported by thick beams that ran from its apex down to the level of the hammocks twelve feet below.

The shaman was already there—Humberto. He was youngish looking, maybe midthirties, about five seven, with wide shoulders and a taut build. He had been conscripted into the Peruvian army and had risen to become its youngest sergeant. Certainly he looked like he was physically capable of handling himself in a tough spot.

Reuben appeared, and Richard introduced him. I was shocked at how thin and pale he was. He had a ghoulish pallor, his skin almost translucent. His chest was practically concave, and he looked close to emaciation. I figured I could completely encircle his upper arms with my finger and thumb. His eyes were the palest blue, huge and unblinking; his sincere and steady gaze emitted a wide-eyed innocence and trust. When he smiled his teeth were a grayish brown. He had a wracking cough that appeared to drain him physically. So *this* is what happens when you live above the Arctic Circle with very little natural light during the winter and abuse drugs intravenously for six months. He had obviously been devastated physically by his addiction, and I wondered what his mental state was like.

Now that everyone was here, we settled ourselves in a semicircle around Humberto, who sat in a rocking chair with its back against the wall. Miley and I chose to lie on mattresses, and Richard and Reuben sat in rocking chairs. Humberto laid out a sort of shrine on a woven mat he placed on the floor a few feet in front of his chair. In the center he placed a Buddha statue and then positioned thirty to forty smaller polished rocks and crystals around it. A clear glass wine bottle full of ayahuasca sat there, brimming with potential. As Humberto called us forward individually, he poured the thick, brown brew into the cup.

I was apprehensive. I had heard that the hallucinogenic brew tasted foul and knew that it was a purgative: thirty minutes after taking it, it's common to have bouts of vomiting.

When my name was called I crawled forward on my hands and knees and accepted the proffered cup. Three or four gulps and it was down, a gloopy brown liquid, disgustingly bitter. Everyone pulled expressions of disgust as they swallowed it. We quickly gulped some water, swilling it around in our mouths in a futile attempt to get rid of the aftertaste. Humberto—a veteran ayahuasca drinker in every sense—grimaced involuntarily after imbibing, and I was surprised to hear him actually groan in displeasure. Clearly this wasn't going to be an acquired taste.

Humberto began singing an *icaro,* and the ceremony began. His voice was strong. Icaros are songs to call in the spirits from the forest and luminal realms. I was feeling disoriented, aware of the near absurdity of my being here, sitting with strangers in the dark in a circle in the jungle, being serenaded by an ayahuasca master, and knowing full well that in a few minutes something extremely strange would be happening.

Each of us had a bucket in case we vomited, and they sat there ominously. Within twenty-five minutes I started to glimpse the merest tickle of something at the edges of my peripheral vision. I tried to ignore it, deny its creeping inevitability. Two minutes later hallucinations came on in full force. I felt a strange energy moving through my body that made me nauseated. Humberto was singing the icaros with ever-increasing vigor, his voice growing louder and clearer, feeding off the ayahuasca energy coursing through him, channeling it.

Incredible geometric shapes swirled kaleidoscopically behind closed eyes. They took on a more deliberate action, swooping wildly into my center of vision and away again, like a swarm of bats, so clear and real that I flinched. They morphed into sleek angular reptilian creatures, swarming, popping out of nowhere, then just as quickly disappearing, only to be replaced by even more almost indescribably bizarre-looking creatures. I still felt lucid and began to hope that it wouldn't get any more intense—it was already beyond strange and who knew where it was leading.

After half an hour, maybe forty minutes, I was in the full grip of the ayahuasca. All the while the icaros had been getting louder and more forceful, and Humberto was shaking two *schacapa* rattles—nothing more than sheaves of thin, dry leaves. He had one in each hand and was waving them vigorously. The effect was a rhythmic swishing sound that became unbelievably loud, adding to the texture of his singing. How on Earth could a bunch of shaking leaves sound so loud? It filled the entire room. All senses on every perceptual level were heightened—maxed out. Too much going on.

An unexpected sense of empathy was growing that became so strong that it felt like a door was opening into a whole new and separate sense—as important and relevant as sight or sound, so powerful it scythed through all other emotions. There was so much more to perceive than just the content of this three-dimensional world. Incapable of resisting any longer, I opened my eyes. *Ka-boom!* The entire room was full of alien life interwoven with a multicolored geometric mesh. Everything everywhere was made of throbbing neon electric grids of energy. The grids entwined with writhing sharp-toothed creatures that scuttled with dazzling, slinky agility. Fractal centipedes and millipedes in iridescent high definition—their glistening, heavily armored bodies trailing off into infinity—encroached. Then with alarming suddenness, they spawned, birthing new hordes of shining exoskeletoid creatures that actually had the audacity to smile. These new creatures' glinty eyes made sure their presence was felt as they confidently claimed their new territory. Then they slunk back to some other-dimensional realm, receding with the same speed and agility. They vanished but, in the very act of disappearing, somehow spawned new creatures, each progeny more strange and alien than its predecessor.

The visions were overwhelming. I was surrounded by fantastical alien beasts, spirits, entities—who knew what the hell they were—that had no physical form. No time for introspection or to rationalize any kind of philosophical interpretation—scenes shifted and morphed with incredible intensity. I struggled to maintain my grip on any kind of ordered thought. How on Earth could this ever be interpreted as therapeutic? Confusion reigned, and I sought some semblance of comfort, unconvincingly forcing myself to think, *Everything will be fine, everything will be fine.*

The sounds of the jungle—insects and frogs—were loud now, and they interwove with the swishing of the schacapa rattles until they reached an all-consuming crescendo that swept me up to ride the waves of a clamorous alien-sounding symphony. Oh my God! These Indians know exactly what they're doing! They had had thousands of years to perfect it. I was journeying through a kind of grotesque, carnivalesque world, and the icaros and leaf rattles were the pilot and navigator. Sounds were *things,* and these things shaped my consciousness, which became as unnavigable as a termite caught in a tornado.

My eyes strained in the darkness. The visible matrixlike energy had a very technical nature, aesthetically pleasing in a very measured and precise way, contrasting with the organic sprawl of the jungle. I remember thinking—*knowing*—that this geometric matrix pattern of multicolored light-energy must be part of life itself, but it was ordinarily hidden by the veil of rational sanity. I had seen these same gridlike patterns in the artwork of the local Shipibo. It was obvious now that these visions had been the inspiration for their art.

In Afghanistan the mantra after each patrol as I lay in bed was "don't think, don't think." Over and over I'd repeat this to myself in an attempt to meditatively anesthetize myself to sleep. Here I was invoking the same technique: "Stop thinking, trying to making sense of it." The message was *surrender*—the exact opposite of everything the military had taught me. *Yield* and allow the visions to flow. Sublime surrender— now I see. Don't fight it, feel it: submission was the solution, ego the enemy. It couldn't get any worse than Helmand, surely? That thought became my grounding rod. This was the connection to an alternative *life force,* and I had jacked into the main vein.

Eventually, after another hour, the icaros stopped. The sounds of creatures in the jungle flooded in to fill the silence. Then I heard Richard's voice.

"Miley?" Richard waited for a response, but none came.

"Miley?" Still nothing. "Miley, are you awake?"

Another few seconds of silence, then he began to speak more forcefully.

"Miley, wake up! Don't sleep! Wake up!"

I couldn't see much in the darkness but heard him rise from his chair and leap over to where Miley was lying on the mattress to my left, only twelve feet away. He knelt down and gently shook her. She was unresponsive, either in deep sleep or unconscious. He shook her gently again, then more vigorously.

"Miley! You must wake up! You must *not* go to sleep. Please, wake up now!"

Humberto came over and joined Richard, trying to awaken her. No good, she remained completely under.

"Very unusual," Richard mumbled, more to himself than to the rest of us.

I could tell he was trying to restrain his concern, but his observation seemed to be the understatement of the century. Incredulously, I thought I heard him say, "She's stopped breathing."

Oh for fuck's sake—just great. My first ayahuasca session, and we have a potential fatality on our hands! I crawled over to them, and the movement brought on fresh waves of nausea. I whispered to Richard, "Can I help?"

"Thanks," he said. "We need to sit her up and keep her in an upright position. She must not be allowed to go to sleep."

It's *way* too late for that, I thought, as I tried lifting her upright. She was an absolute dead weight, and I had to kneel behind her to get leverage. I held her in a sitting position with my palms spread across the span of her back at the shoulder blades and her weight supported against me. She was still out of it, her head slumped forward, chin against her chest and eyes closed. I couldn't hear her breathing.

Richard asked for a torch, and I reached with one hand into my pocket and gave him my little Maglite. He shone it at her face, but there was no reaction from her whatsoever. For the next ten minutes, Richard and I took turns propping Miley upright or massaging her back. He peeled her eyelids back with his thumbs, and under the harsh light it was ugly. Her pupils engulfed her irises entirely. Huge, black, and empty; I'd never seen anything like it. This must be what catatonia is. In an effort to stimulate her, Humberto blew tobacco smoke over her head. In the Amazon this pure jungle tobacco is a healing remedy. The smoke from these thick hand-rolled cigarettes, called *mapachos,* is used in rituals as a cleansing agent, supposedly clearing a person's field of bad energy. Richard confirmed she was still breathing.

Humberto and Richard conferred quietly, muttering ominously together in Spanish. Richard finally turned to Miley and spoke to her somewhat self-consciously, the way you might speak to someone in a coma. "OK, Miley. Humberto is going to sing you a special icaro. He's going to *sing* you back to us. You *will* wake up and you *will* come back." Humberto began to sing loudly, infusing the song with his entire life force. I'd never heard anything like it—so powerful and alien.

From the darkness Reuben called out. "Richard? Richard! What are you doing? Why aren't you here next to me?"

I was gobsmacked—did he actually just say that? For the first and only time, I heard Richard speak tersely, a strained tension in his voice. "Reuben, I'm with Miley. She needs our help! If you're not going to help, then at least be quiet!"

My arms were aching from bearing Miley's weight. Richard said, "I appreciate your help."

"No problem. This is what we do, right?" I said, sweating bullets, peering through the darkness and failing to meet his gaze.

At least she was breathing; we knew that much. After nearly half an hour of massaging her back and Humberto singing to her and encouraging her return, Humberto announced that she was going to be fine. We should now let her sleep. We laid her down carefully on the mattress and went back to our own spots in the semicircle around Humberto's chair. He resumed his singing for the group. Every ten minutes or so, we took turns checking on Miley. She was breathing steadily, and if we shook her, she groaned quietly. Thank God.

With Miley taken care of, Humberto was soon asleep in his rocking chair. Richard wandered off to go and sleep in his bed, leaving just Reuben and me. We chatted quietly, and as we did, Miley awakened and unsteadily rose from the mattress. She tried to walk toward the toilets but was wobbly and in danger of falling. I rushed over to steady her, and as she put her weight on me, I nearly toppled over, unsteady from the lingering effects of the ayahuasca. Propping her up from beneath her armpits, I practically dragged her to the toilet. She tried to say something but could barely talk. When we got there I made sure she had a torch and knew where the toilet paper was, then pulled the curtain and went back across the room to the mattress, lay down, and fell asleep.

Waking up four hours later, the light of the Amazon dawn flooded in through the gauze of the wraparound window. A quick glance at the mattress to my left revealed that Miley was missing. I stumbled groggily to the toilets and found her in the same cubicle where she'd been left hours before. She was lying on the cold tile floor huddled in a fetal position, fast asleep, surrounded by vomit. I cleaned up the mess and shook her awake as gently as I could.

"Miley, you've fallen asleep in the toilet."

She mumbled something unintelligible and laughed, embarrassed. Jesus Christ, this has really knocked her out. There was a strong likelihood that this was the most undignified and out of it she'd ever been in her life. Certainly, from the conversations we'd had, I knew she led a conservative lifestyle, and this current state was way beyond her realm of experience.

I got her back to her room and in bed, returned to my room, and lay down for some proper shut-eye. I could still feel the visionary plant medicine coursing in my system, and the feeling was now calm serenity.

I hoped the next ceremony would go a little easier on all of us.

13

Jungle Wonder

The next day Richard, Humberto, Reuben, and I sat talking over breakfast. Humberto suspected, as did Richard, that a dark energy had entered Miley and lodged deep within her to bring on the catatonic episode. Richard euphemistically called it a "funky energy."

Whatever the cause, Humberto was confident that whatever the dark energy or disembodied entity was that had invaded her, he could remove it completely given a couple of weeks of ceremonies and concerted shamanic healing effort. It was obvious to Humberto that this energy was more than just funky. I felt almost certain that in his private conversations with Richard, which I had overheard, Humberto had used the word *demonio,* Spanish for demon.

Reuben seemed to fall asleep between mouthfuls during lunch, his head bobbing comically up and down. We all wanted to know if Miley had any recollection of her catatonic experience. Not surprisingly, what little she remembered was hazy. She had heard us calling her name and was aware of us trying to wake her up. She thought that she had responded; while we had been near panic, she had felt fine and calm. This was good news, and we didn't go into any more detail of our experience of the previous night. With plenty more ceremonies to participate in, no one wanted to antagonize anything that had been stirred up in her.

Later that afternoon Miley and I got to know each other better. I showed her a downloaded YouTube clip called *Double Rainbow,* a popular meme watched more than forty-two million times. It shows a man in America and the double rainbow that appeared over his front yard. He freaks out in humbled awe, equally touching and hilarious.

I left the room to wander around the perimeter of the encampment, peering into the vegetation as the evening drew in. The jungle—the polar opposite of civilized, like a mystical sage who didn't care what the hell ordinary folk thought. It was going to do its own thing whether we existed or not. It was verdant, inconceivably dense, mighty, and so mysterious. Truth be told, at times it was intimidating.

I walked to the waterfall. There was a faint rainbow several meters wide in the mist. Hummingbirds flitted among the flowers, reminding me of something I had once heard: "Hummingbirds are the nerve endings of God." I stripped off, stepping beneath the pounding torrent. Freezing water crashed, snatching my breath away, pummeling my head and shoulders like a brutal masseuse. I had to breathe out forcefully, trying to bear the enormous weight of the water. The gasps grew louder and louder until I found myself roaring, like a beast, an ape who roars because it feels so right. And yet even the roaring was drowned out by the thundering waterfall. The effect of the release was fantastically cleansing, a year of hardship washed away in the torrent of sound and water. As I got dressed a huge blue butterfly landed on my patrol pack.

Dusk fell and we gathered in the maloca and readied ourselves for the second ceremony. We sat in a semicircle around Humberto. Everyone was pensive, except for Richard and Humberto, who joked in Spanish and laughed. Miley had elected not to drink any ayahuasca this evening. Secretly I was relieved.

Humberto began to sing the icaros as we went up, one by one, raising the cup and saying *"Salud!"* before gulping down the bitter, foul-tasting brew. We settled back in our places and waited for the fun and games to begin.

I felt nauseated almost immediately. Richard reminded us that vomiting is not looked upon with any kind of embarrassment or shame; it is a natural part of the ayahuasca healing process. In this context purging helps to release stuck emotions such as shame, fear, and guilt and to clear out cellular detritus.

Reuben retched loudly into his bucket. It sounded painful and seemed to go on for several minutes, each heave sounding utterly inhuman, emanating from the core animal part of himself that was way beyond caring about decorum, esteem, or any other fancy civilized constructs. The sound of his retching was likely to provoke the same response in me. Sure enough, I soon found myself undergoing an onslaught. I grabbed my bucket and emptied the very dregs of my stomach into it. My head was deep in the bucket, and my muffled moans were amplified as they resonated around the inside of the bucket and back out again. I didn't care. Reuben had started the pukefest and I was on the tag team. This was Reuben's twentieth ayahuasca session over nearly as many nights, and all of a sudden my view of him changed. I had respect for what he must have gone through. I now saw him not as a weak, addicted young man but as a veteran upchucker and, more importantly, as a champion, someone who stuck with it, even when the "it" is energy sapping and mind blowing. *If this kid can survive this twenty times, I can get through it tonight.*

Reuben's purging sounded particularly agonizing. Between retches, he made faint feminine-sounding childlike gasps in an effort to catch his breath, making my heart wrench. Jesus, that poor boy! He needs healing. I couldn't help but wonder what he had endured in his short life. As he continued to expel the contents of his guts, I did my best to send him supportive energy through the ether, hoping his discomfort would quickly pass. No chance. After what must have been the tenth bout of vomiting, he sounded absolutely wiped out. He was still struggling to catch his breath, just about managing to make the delicate sighs of a dying elderly lady, too weak now to even groan. I tried to approach the purging as matter-of-factly as Richard did. Get it out, get it over with, move on. Before long even Richard had joined in the puke chorus, a bona-fide ayahuasca veteran, and his retching didn't sound any less painful than the rest of us.

With my vomiting over, feeling thoroughly drained, I settled back. A sense of serenity swept over me like warm a bath. The contrast was perplexing. I felt peaceful, cared for, as if ayahuasca were a mother stroking her child's hair, calming, a cleansed and soothing release.

The brew wound its way through my system as I rocked gently to and fro in a wire mesh rocking chair. I could barely make out Richard's and Reuben's faint silhouettes in the darkness. Miley appeared to be asleep on the mattress to my left. The familiar sensation of boundaries dissolving. All physical limits lost their significance as I became absorbed into an infinite fabric, hitherto unseen, but now startlingly apparent. I was astonished at the clarity of the visions that seemed to originate in my mind's eye, perhaps the third eye of esoteric lore, as dormant neurons became illuminated as the ceremony unraveled. Tendrils of colored light connected everything to everything in a cosmic web from which new realities emerged. Objects shone with a vividness and clarity beyond even our best HD technology. Somehow my own mind was manifesting bright white light. Inner landscapes were geometric, and I intuited a mathematical underpinning to everything. Geometry was the great connective tissue of the universe. My mind now wired, fired, and inspired. A cosmic reset was unfolding, a latent sense now activated, humming at exquisite levels of sensitivity like a heavy curtain had been raised to reveal—ta da!—the *real* real. There was humor in this intelligence; ayahuasca was like a magician pulling a rabbit out of a hat. There was a burgeoning sense of awakening as if the *real* nature of reality has been a secret guarded by elites and holy men throughout history and now I had become an initiate, a sense of awe, beyond wonder at the majesty of it all. Was *this* potion the source of a power knowledge that could be harnessed for both good and bad?

I was now fully connected. Connected to others, to nature, and, if there is such an entity, to the Source, feeling the presence of what I can only describe as holiness. On the spectrum of holy sensations, I felt "grind your forehead into the floorboards, outstretched arms, palms and face down, backside in the air" holy. A sense of utter surrender and worship. I felt love so deep that, for the first time ever, all I could *do* was worship. And of course I didn't even know what I was worshipping! It had no name, no form—just pure, pure ineffable *devotion*.

Every single thing in existence that could be conceived and perceived—the lowliest to the highest, the most mundane to the most magnificent—was all bathed in this holiness. It was energy—a power, external and independent, a creative animating life force. The sacred Amazonian vine had delivered an experience that was truly, truly mystical.

Humberto walked over and stood before me, his body less than a foot away from my face. He began to sing. I could barely make out his silhouette it was so dark, but the *power* he imparted through his voice and this song felt all consuming—beyond mere human passion! I was subsumed into his emanating aura. *Radiate, radiate, radiate,* the words tumbled over and over in my mind.

Awed, I sat upright, but with my head bowed low. My hands were moving, seemingly independent of any conscious thought, alternating between two prayer positions, one with fingers entwined, hands clasped together, and the other with my fingers steepled, fingertips lightly touching in the classic prayer position. Dear God and Jesus Christ, *please*—what is happening to me? I felt humbled, although this massively understates the depth of my feeling. I had never experienced anything like this phantasmagoria overload. A master *ayahuasquero* was singing healing energy into me in the pitch blackness, a melodic foghorn in human form, hallucinatory images swirling around us, through us. A personal serenade from Pavarotti wouldn't have come close. I could see, hear, and feel the sacredness of nature. I realized that our constitution is infused with a dualism that makes us a divine but self-destructing species, that we only exist at all thanks entirely to the whim and grace of nature. I began to understand that I was being made to feel, regardless of my own intentions, and whether I liked it or not, inspired. The sanctity and profundity were indescribable. I knew I would never be the same again. I'd been clubbed into higher sentience by an ancient wisdom so radiant it was humiliating. Laughing voices from forgotten epochs seemed to say, "That'll learn him! Behold *this,* dummy! How does it feel to have your confidence mashed? Where's it now, eh? Cocky bastard, weren't you?"

Humberto stepped back, sparked up a mapacho, and leaned in closer, blowing a thick cloud of tobacco smoke over the top of my head, another one across my chest, and another down my back. He exhaled the smoke with a force that sounded completely inhuman, and I could tell by the vibration in his voice that he physically shivered and shook as he did so, his exertion primitive and primal. I felt blessed to be the recipient of his ministrations.

When he was done I asked Richard to translate for me. "Please tell the maestro that I believe he truly *is* a maestro."

Humberto then moved over to where Miley was lying on the mattress and began to perform a healing. Reuben was next. Humberto performed with the same vigor with each of them. As he did this I felt my hands once again take on a life of their own, forming spontaneously into a prayer position. I had no idea why they were doing this, although the room was bathed in reverence and the prayer position felt the most natural and comfortable position for my hands to be in. The sense of being awash in divinity, an unfathomable holiness, permeated every facet of my being. I now understood why the indigenous peoples of this region revered ayahuasca. There was power here. This was the end of faith for me. Faith was redundant, a quaint anachronism, relegated to whimsy, the runt in the litter of dogged conviction. Just drink a cup of *this* and compare *that* to where faith gets you.

Reuben asked Richard to translate for him. "Can you ask the shaman if my mother is OK?" he asked. "Is she well?"

"Why?" asked Richard.

"Because I can feel her," he explained, "and I'm worried about her." He paused, then repeated in a voice sounding like a frightened little boy, "Is she safe?"

My heart ached listening to him.

"OK, wait a moment . . ." I heard Richard whisper something to Humberto. There was silence for about a minute, and then Humberto spoke softly to Richard in Spanish, who translated. "The maestro says your mother is safe. She is well. Don't worry."

"Thank you, maestro. Thank you," Reuben said in a voice barely audible but full of relief.

We all sat in silence, in complete peace. Peace on Earth. It was real. Real peace, here deep, deep in the Amazon. The most tranquil hour of my life unfolded ineffably. *Now* was all that mattered, can matter, and will ever matter. This very perfect moment right now.

The ceremony had been a cosmic liftoff from the start, and now hours later, as it was coming to a close, it was blissful. I was more confident than ever that there is more to existence than our five physical senses allow us to perceive. That there is *no* limit to our perceptual capacities was the epiphany. I could now understand why people who have near-death experiences say they are irrevocably changed for the better. DMT and ayahuasca delivered those life-changing moments. I had just directly experienced that spirituality is just physics that we haven't yet understood. Many people already knew this; I was just waking up.

Richard was keen to bring to South America what he'd learned from three years living in India and Thailand. He was combining continental wisdoms. He meditated by the river every morning. He told us about a special type of ayurvedic breathing technique that enhanced the feelings generated by ayahuasca. He said when he was practicing this breathing technique while under the influence of ayahuasca, he had became aware of an energy spinning in all of his chakra centers. A spinning ball of light had broken out from one of the chakras and whizzed up and down his body, from one chakra point to another. He said it was the most amazingly ecstatic feeling he'd ever experienced.

But other incidents occurred while I was staying there that made me realize this place could be dangerous—maybe not as dangerous as

Afghanistan but still plenty to be aware of. It would have been naïve to arrive with expectations of sanitized safety. One of them occurred the next day.

Richard asked us if we would like to go on a boat trip along one of the backwater rivers that led to a large freshwater lake. Although we were all relatively weak from the shamanic diet and lack of sleep, this sounded like an opportunity not to be missed. Miley, Reuben, Richard, and I piled into the homemade motorized canoe. Humberto joined us, along with the young local man who helped to make the ayahuasca.

We chugged along at about five miles an hour for nearly an hour. The jungle grew thick, right up to the banks on both sides of the river. I felt free and unburdened, enjoying the ride, intoxicated by the landscape, trailing one hand languidly in the warm crystal-clear freshwater. Every once in a while we'd see flashes of color pop in the green of the jungle, and Richard slipped effortlessly into a naturalist's role, naming the tropical birds. Eventually, we entered a channel so narrow that the vegetation pressed into us from the banks. We had to use our arms to keep the branches out of our faces. The landscape changed again, the water channel opening into swamp terrain. We were surrounded by open water, with no solid land in sight. Plants were growing in clumps here and there, gnarly rooted and partially submerged, extending deep into the mud bottom that was at least ten feet below the waterline.

Then we got stuck. The propeller got caught in a discarded fishing net. We were miles from anywhere, no land to walk on and no way of communicating. A couple of us had mobile phones, but they were useless. We didn't even have a spare paddle. Literally up a creek without one. I never imagined I would actually be in *that* situation. Humberto struggled for five minutes or so, trying in vain to free the propeller. I broke out my lock knife and offered it. Within a minute we were free and moving once more.

I was incredulous. I was supposed to be the dumb tourist here! Where was Richard's knife? Or Humberto's? Or anyone else's? This was the Amazon for Christ's sake. We were deep, deep in the jungle, God knows where in fact, and no one apart from me had thought to pack a knife or any other kind of emergency provisions. That little three-inch blade saved our collective bacon that day. "Carry a knife—save a life," indeed! I had my patrol pack with me. Stuffed at the very bottom was a basic jungle survival kit that I had cobbled together from a marine recipe and a couple of others pulled from the Internet the week before the trip. I hadn't mentioned it to Richard or any of the others because I'd have been embarrassed if they'd teased me about "preparation overkill." But the irony was that without that knife we'd have needed every single item in the survival kit over the next few days as we waited, hoping to be rescued. The jungle is no benign oasis, a beautiful mirage; you still need to pay attention. This is not some la-la land. The natural power here can extinguish you like a draft on a lit match.

Not long after our return to the camp, it was time to gather for the next ceremony. As we sat in a semicircle around Humberto, having already taken the foul brew and waiting for its effects, I heard Reuben groan and say, "Oh, I feel so *full* of ayahuasca! I need a break."

This was his twenty-third ayahuasca ceremony in nearly as many consecutive nights, and I sympathized. Soon enough, Reuben was purging, and when he seemed to have emptied himself completely, he again inquired about his mother's well-being. Humberto assured him she was fine, and Reuben settled down, although he occasionally erupted in wracking coughs that sounded horrendously painful.

Suddenly, the village dogs started barking. Humberto leapt out of his rocking chair and ran over to the window. He shouted something in Spanish to Richard, and then in the near darkness of the maloca, his eyes wide, he ran and grabbed one of the three rifles that were propped against a wall by the door. In an instant, Richard was by his side, and just before he ran from the maloca, he stopped to throw me what looked like an ancient musket. "Here, use this if you have to!" he said, and then he disappeared after Humberto into the night.

I had to stop myself from laughing. A *musket!* I squinted down, inspecting it more carefully and realized it wasn't quite as primitive a firearm, but not by much. I checked the breach—empty. I remembered seeing some shotgun cartridges lined up on the window ledge, so I staggered over, lurching at every step, and grabbed a handful, stuffing them into my pocket. The loading procedure on this weapon couldn't have been any simpler—just shove a cartridge into the barrel and snap it shut. No safety catch, so it's good to go. But what good would it do? The weapon had to be a hundred years old. If I pulled the trigger, the barrel might burst open, peeling back like a banana skin.

The gun was up and ready, the butt tucked firmly into my shoulder. I peered into the jungle, covering the two men already out on the ground, and wondered what the threat could be. I figured it was either bandits or a jaguar, and I didn't know which of those possibilities I preferred. My blurred vision was straining in the darkness. The dogs were still going crazy, barking and running around the perimeter of the camp where it met the jungle. I was unsteady on my feet and still hallucinating hard. A threat to our lives—this was the last thing I expected. I hadn't come all the way from Afghanistan to get killed by bandits in a gunfight in the Amazon, or for that matter, eaten alive by a big jungle cat. I realized that up until now, I'd hardly seen the wilder side of Peru.

Out the window I could see Humberto holding his torch parallel with his rifle barrel, the gun tucked in his shoulder, while he patrolled along the edge of the jungle, switching from shaman to soldier.

I stumbled out through the door and into the night, the safety of the lodge behind me, my mind racing. You have got to be fucking joking. I'm off my tits here, probably about to tackle a beast that tears lesser animals to pieces with its very *face,* while I'm having, like it or not, some kind of communion with an unknowable Oversoul entity—and now you're laying *this* on me? Come on!

I glanced up from peering down the barrel to see Richard waving his arm wildly, gesturing that I should move around the perimeter in the opposite direction to him. We parted, stalking in opposing directions—he moved right, I skirted around to the left. One of the dogs rushed past me on my left shoulder and stopped at the edge of the last hut, barking into the blackness of the camp perimeter. The lights from the camp didn't extend more than five meters into the jungle. My eyes were straining, and then I saw it—a beast of a cat, magnificent! It's coat just like a leopard's, its eyes big and wide staring right back at me, no trace of fear. Fuck me.

"Richard, it's here. Jaguar! Over here. I think it's a young one," I hissed.

I brought the barrel up and took aim. A wishful thought flashed: more than anything, right now I wanted one of the zombie-killer pump-action shotguns we'd used in Afghanistan. No chance. But by this time Richard and Humberto were both by my side. I nodded toward the fallen log at the jungle's edge that the jaguar crouched behind. They followed my gaze, then burst out laughing.

"It's an ocelot! An ocelot, and it's not even full-grown!" said Richard.

Humberto was pissing himself with laughter, saying something in Spanish in between his cackles. I lowered the barrel of the shotgun and looked at Richard sheepishly. "What's he saying," I asked, nodding toward the shaman.

"He said no one ever got harmed by an ocelot, *hombre,* and that you look like you just shit yourself."

Not fair. How was I supposed to know the difference when I'm tripping my balls off on some crazy hallucinogenic jungle juice? Bastards. Richard joined in the laughter with Humberto, both of them exchanging jokes in Spanish.

"What's he saying now?" I asked Richard.

He had no answer, or chose not to tell me. Quite clearly the joke was on me. I looked back toward the jungle and the "big" wild cat was gone.

No bandits, no jaguar—an ocelot. Richard and Humberto were still giggling like idiots as we returned to the lodge. We all settled back down into our places and resumed the ceremony. Within minutes it was like nothing had happened. Humberto was singing his heart out, and the icaros were doing their job of massaging our consciousness and shifting the visions.

I know Richard had our best interests at heart, but this place was no picnic, and it had a kind of Wild West feel about it.

Reuben was intelligent, unquestionably the brightest nineteen-year-old I'd ever met. Norwegian was his native language, but he was fluent in English, approaching fluency in Spanish, and could get by in French. He was extremely well read and had an encyclopedic knowledge of all sorts of authors of esoteric books and their theories. Terence McKenna, Eckhart Tolle, George Orwell, hermeticism, gnosticism, alchemy, the ancient Greek Elysian mysteries—he knew about them all, and he had learned most of it from the Internet. He was full of amusing witticisms and nuggets of wisdom. "Worrying is just the unnecessary investment of the imagination" was one of my favorites.

But his graphic description of his addiction was disturbing. He had had a chronic skunk (strong marijuana) addiction while also intravenously abusing ketamine and amphetamines—every single day. For more than a year he'd maintained this lifestyle: doing drugs and hardly eating anything or seeing anybody. His descriptions of the comedowns from the highs, curled in a fetal position and wracked by involuntary shakes and shivers for up to five hours, sounded horrendous. I asked him the obvious question, but I was still curious to hear his answer. "Your parents must have told you that if you inject recreational drugs intravenously it's a one-way ticket to the Badlands?"

"Yeah," he deadpanned, "they told me. But I did it anyway."

Eventually, he had reached rock bottom emotionally and physically. He stumbled across information about ayahuasca as a therapy to help treat drug addiction and decided that this was his way back to sanity and freedom. His mother had accompanied him to South America, handed him over to Richard, and flown back to Norway. So here he was, getting clean. As Reuben told us his story, his voice broke and croaked, as if he were a tired old man. His addictions had sapped the energy from him. I compared him with the young marines I had served with, marveling at how different human beings can be. I had no doubt that a comparison of Reuben's physical capability compared to marines of the same age would have been pitiful. But he was certainly deeper than most of them philosophically.

During one of the quieter, reflective moments in a ceremony, Reuben asked Richard if he would say a prayer. Richard said, "Sure," and immediately in his warm baritone voice prayed aloud:

> *Om, Almighty, Omnipresent, Loving Father, I am your humble son, Thy will be done. Please guide us now to the Light of Truth and shine away the darkness of egoic illusion. Please cause all bodies to vibrate at the frequency of Love, dissolving all impediments to the natural, spontaneous, free, direct experience and expression of Your unconditional divine Love. Please guide our little wills to be aligned at all times with Your divine will, Father, causing every thought, word, deed to be in service to the greatest and highest good of all life everywhere.*
>
> *I am love, for this I am in truth. I am light, I am love.*
>
> *I am the power and the peace of light. I radiate these qualities in all directions to all beings across all times, dimensions, and planes for the upliftment of the whole, that all Your children, our brothers and sisters, may find their way home to You, Father.*
>
> *For I have learned the folly of these ways and know now from experience that in and of the little self there is no power and certainly no peace, for All unfolds only by virtue of Your divine grace and presence; the true immortal Self.*
>
> *Therefore we pray for You to guide us from illusion to truth, from ignorance to wisdom, from darkness to light, and from death into immortality, for Yours is the only Power, Light, and Love illuminating the way, Father.*

Blessings be unto one and all, for all are one and one is all.

Om Namah Shivaya. Om mani padme hum. Om shanti, shanti, shanti om! Gloria in excelsis deo!

Reading the words of this prayer now, starkly on the page, diminishes the power that they had at the time I actually heard them. The three of us were bathed in an aura of union and grace. Upon hearing the request, Richard had delivered the prayer spontaneously, tenderly, without a moment's hesitation. There in the darkness, with ayahuasca lingering in our systems, senses heightened, and our hearts open, the prayer carried a power and beauty that I believed could have the potential to resonate with anyone, of any faith.

During the ceremonies Richard's mind was lucid compared to my inability to hold the simplest of thoughts consistently for more than few seconds. His mental acuity seemed near perfect. Evidently, his longtime use of ayahuasca hadn't adversely impacted his ability to concentrate. He and Humberto were both exemplars that the use of entheogens could be successfully assimilated into everyday life.

We sat for a while in silence and contemplation. In this place and at moments like these, I realized we shared something sacred. I *felt* it. Something was happening to me. I was changing.

During the ceremonies I quickly fell into a routine of contemplation while waiting for the onset of the visions. After drinking the brew I'd spend twenty to thirty minutes meditating on all the things for which I was grateful: My wife. My children. Friends. My physical health. My mental health. My relationship with my best friend of thirty years. My mother. My rekindled relationship with my biological father. My dog. The five senses that bring me so much pleasure. My country (Great Britain—politically and geologically stable, no earthquakes, tornadoes, tsunamis). My good fortune with work. My attitude toward life. My attitude toward death. My neighbors and community. The experiences I'd had while traveling to so many places around the world. The

Internet. My ability to make friends. My experiences with ayahuasca and psilocybin—glimpses into an awesome cosmos. Delicious food to eat every day. Freedom to go wherever I want and to think and speak whatever I want. The ability to work from home. Support from everyone I meet. A bright future. The fifty days a year when the weather is beautiful where I live. A family history to be proud of. The list went on and on. I could easily spend half an hour listing all the things I was grateful for, by which time the ayahuasca would begin taking effect.

After two weeks of ceremonies, it was time for me to leave. Richard was the real deal. On the final night Humberto had said that he thought I was "good." Meaning, I think, that my energy was relatively clean. I was pleased to get this shamanic tick in the box and felt that I could move on to the next stage of discovery. The Mythic Voyage sounded like an opportunity too good to miss—its pull nothing less than gravitational on a planetary scale. It shone like a lighthouse illuminating the way to more mystery, mysticism, and mind-melding weirdness. Count me in. After all, after what I had already been through, what could possibly go wrong?

The day before departure I was lying in a hammock reading, when I heard Reuben shout, "Alex, come and see this!" I trotted up in my shorts and flip-flops and saw that he was gazing up, grinning at the sky. I followed his gaze and could hardly believe what I was seeing. A double rainbow. A double rainbow right here in the jungle! My first. So beautiful—a marvel. And a synchronicity since I had started this trip with the YouTube video and had shared it with Miley.

For me there was now an unshakable conviction that the ayahuasca ceremonies developed by the Shipibo were some kind of portal to a new level of consciousness, as if dormant antenna neurons had been activated. This was not merely another drug, a diversion. To call this special tea that the Natives brewed a "drug" was an abomination. It was more like a kind of technology.

In the Hindu tradition the Creator or Universal Intelligence—the

Source and Essence of everything—is called Brahma; in the Judeo-Christian tradition, God; in one of many Chinese traditions, the Tao. Here in the Amazon regions, it is the Forest Mother. The creator spirit is feminine. In the fecundity of the rainforest, this is no surprise. I was beginning to become deeply attached to the Amazon. Looking at that double rainbow, I became acutely aware of how we in the West generally cut ourselves off from nature and spirit. We live in cities—everything is increasingly man-made and nature is kept at a distance. We have lost our affinity for the spiritual aspects of nature. We are detached from the Source as an organic spiritual presence in everyday life. The Amazon seemed to vibrate with energy, and it was impossible not to be impressed and affected by it.

14

Journey to the Middle of Nowhere

I kicked back in Iquitos for a couple of days after leaving La Kapok Center. Taking advantage of the phone reception, I called home each day to check all was well and then mooched about the markets on the edge of the shantytown. Andreas was the name of the Greek man who conceived, led, and delivered the Mythic Voyage, and I looked forward to meeting him and the other mythic voyagers (whom I soon learned Andreas refered to as argonauts).

While having breakfast in a café overlooking the river, a young man approached me selling trinkets and crystals. He had no idea I was working with ayahuasca, yet said solemnly, "Everyone in the world needs ayahuasca. It will help save the world."

He picked one of the largest and clearest quartz crystals from his cache and held it quite firmly to my temple. "Can you feel that?" he asked. "Can you *feel* it?"

Beads of sweat covered his brow; his eyes were wide and intense. I admitted that I didn't feel anything but was intrigued by the claim that you could potentially feel the power of crystalline rock just by holding it in close proximity to your head. He told me he'd been training as a shaman for seven years, although he made it clear he couldn't begin to express how difficult that apprenticeship had been. His face looked filled with the world's woes as he stressed, "It has been a hard journey. So hard, so, so hard."

He turned to leave, put his hands together in a prayer position, and bowed his head. "I feel you," he said softly. "I feel you are a good person. Peace be upon you, brother." Then he walked away.

He probably said that to all the travelers who bought his trinkets. I shook my head in bewilderment.

I checked into the Trek hotel for my last night in Iquitos. The next day I would be meeting with Andreas and his "argonauts." According to his website:

> The intention is for a collective vibration of openness, light and goodwill creating new friends, travellers on the paths of the warriors of light. This however is not a touristic voyage, although we do have an awesome time; it is meant for people who, however good their lives have been up to now, want more out of their lives, people who wish to be free to be anyone they want and live any way they wish, people who wish to dream new lives into being and a new, full of light world.
>
> Ayahuasca . . . can offer what has been called "ten years of psychotherapy in one night," giving the possibility of a direct communication and conversation with our subconscious, with total and unrestricted access to all our memories and events of our lives as well as our cellular memories, a totally clear and lucid mind and a spectacular visual journey that can heal deep wounds, liberate from addictions, give clarity and purpose and expand our consciousness.

It all sounded intriguing. While checking in I met one of the other argonauts in the lobby. She introduced herself as Anna, and we went to dinner. She was a location scout for a Czech film company. This was her second Mythic Voyage, and her eyes filled with wonder as she assured me this was no ordinary journey. In an effort to mask my naïveté, I countered with some La Kapok Center anecdotes. She reciprocated with the smile of a mother for a son who had just learned to tie his shoelaces. We said good night, and her parting words were, "Just you wait."

Excitement bubbled up. I got back to the room and noticed its ramshackle state. Dark, dingy—in dire need of modernization. The spartan room, with its single bed, was poorly lit. No window, no natural light. The walls were painted brown, and the weakest of lamplights cast eerie shadows. A coal black TV set protruded from an extendable bracket high up on the opposite wall facing the bed, crouching like a gargoyle waiting to pounce.

The introductory meeting for the argonauts was at seven o'clock the next night in the same hotel. About twenty people already sat on chairs in a large circle in the hotel conference room. Andreas stood up to greet me, beaming. In his early fifties and huge, six feet four and quite possibly the same in circumference—at least three hundred pounds. His waist was gargantuan. His head was shaved, and he sported a goatee beard. He greeted me warmly. "Alex. You've arrived. It's good for you to come here and join us."

There was no questioning his sincerity. The room held a diverse bunch of voyagers, late teens to fifties and sixties. Andreas launched into his welcome speech.

"Argonauts, welcome to the Mythic Voyage!"

His voice boomed, loud as a triumphant medieval monarch proclaiming victory in battle. Hotel staff, waiting in the wings with refreshments, shot each other nervous glances. In a voice as oversized as his body, he explained that we were going on a journey into the deepest parts of the jungle. Our characters would be tested, and we would need to trust each other, trust him, and trust his team. This was the sixth Mythic Voyage, and there were several people who had participated three, four, even five times before. Each new setting for a ceremony in the jungle would produce a new unique effect. He assured us that we'd discover the power of intention and go inside ourselves using ayahuasca to heal, evolve, and transform.

We paid our money and decamped en masse to a nearby restaurant, incongruously named The Texan Rose. We sat around a long table that comfortably accommodated all twenty of us, snaffling the last supper down our necks. I sat in the middle on one side, able to peer along each side of the table to both my left and right. Some were traveling solo, others in groups of two, three, or more. I sat opposite a young man and woman, Trey and Belinda, who were part of a group of Australians in their twenties. Ruth, Belinda's twin, sat farther down the table. They had a hippie sensibility in their clothes and jewelery, right down to Belinda and her sister having long, fair hair on their legs and armpits.

We tucked into the food, and Andreas informed us that it would be our last indulgent meal for at least a week, as we would be starting the ayahuasca diet right away—meaning just vegetables, boiled rice, fruit, no seasonings or condiments. Only two small bland meals a day.

Everyone was upbeat the next morning as we rode by bus to board the beautifully restored nineteenth-century riverboat. There were two main decks, with twelve two-berth cabins on the lower deck. The upper deck had an expansive lounging area where everyone tended to hang out and most of the socializing took place.

I explored the ship, impressively restored to its old-world charm, with many original period fittings. The dining room on the lower deck was luxuriously decorated. In the center of the room was a huge, dark wood table that could seat twenty-four people. On the upper deck, there was a small, plush library.

As we set sail Andreas flamboyantly shouted, "Argonauts! You are all now fucked! Because you are all now mine!"

He paused, looking into the eyes of each of us, and said, "We are going on a journey miles from anywhere, and you have to trust me." He smiled. Most people laughed, soaking up the theatrics. To me it sounded a little ominous. He intended to use psychoactive plant medicines in shamanic ceremonies. The only one to be genuinely concerned about was datura, used for centuries in some cultures as a deadly poison, although it has been known to be used in tiny quantities for its psycho-active properties by some shamans. Vice.com had filmed a documentary on datura called *Colombian Devil's Breath*—something to avoid at all costs.

Expectations were high and the weather ideal, so I wandered around to the front of the ship to enjoy the view. There I came upon a young man, alone, standing in the premium position, right at the apex of the bow. The river was over a mile wide, and the full panorama presented itself as glorious river, forest, and sky, truly breathtaking. I approached him smiling, holding out my hand and introducing myself, and he greeted me warmly. His name was Phil, one of the Australian party, twenty-seven years old, conspicuously good looking, with a Jim Morrison haircut and three weeks of stubble. I assumed he must be an actor or something similar but obviously didn't ask. This was his fourth Mythic Voyage. We were quiet, admiring the stunning vista painted with the most exquisite clouds I'd ever seen. It seemed appropriate to offer up some kind of appreciative comment, but when I spoke, it sounded con-trived, spluttering, "I'm really appreciating the sky and clouds today and looking forward to enjoying more of them while on this trip." Quite possibly the dorkiest thing I've ever said out loud. I managed to make myself cringe in self-sabotage. A voice in my head shouted, "No! Stop talking before you damage yourself forever."

No need to panic. He turned to face me, his eyes shut, seemingly wincing slightly in response to a minor pain. Shaking his head ever so gently, he said, "Oh, man!" He screwed his eyes even more tightly shut. "Oh, man. Oh, man." Then he put his hand on my shoulder. Barely audible, deliberately slowly, he whispered, "Dude. You honestly have absolutely *no* idea how beautiful it can get. Believe me."

A reasonable prophecy, in fact completely correct. All I knew was in that moment, in the now, with the breeze on my face and the sky and river so lush and vivid, it was intoxicating. Like the sandstorm in the desert the night before our insertion by Chinook chopper into the front line—the cusp of adventure. Caught up in the spirit of the moment and in the clumsiest way, I blurted out, "You know what? I've never let anybody down." Then I paused. "Well, not in any significant way. Not ever."

What a dickhead. Really? Who says that shit to a person he's just met? Why be compelled to gush like that? The result was embarrassment for oversharing of the highest order. At some unconscious level I was desperate to create a good first impression but instead sounded like a needy little bitch. What is someone supposed to say in response? "Oh, well done. And would you mind terribly if I gave you a round of applause?" When, what they were really thinking was, "You liar."

Without missing a beat, and bless his gentlemanly heart, all Phil said was, "Yes. But have you ever let *yourself* down?"

A perfect gotcha.

Looking down at the deck, I replied sheepishly, "All the time. All the time."

He grinned, and we stood in silence immersed in the view. I had been affected by the recent time invested at La Kapok Center. I wanted to connect and engage with other people on a deeper level. Antisocial boundaries and English reserve were crumbling as I felt a stronger immediate affinity with each new person I met.

I went to my cabin, curious to meet my new bunkmate. Panos was tall and gangly—about thirty-five—and wore tiny oval glasses and had a pointy goatee and straggly, shoulder-length hair. A socks-with-sandals kind of guy. Romanian, a photographer, married, with a four-year-old daughter. He came from a quiet rural area and seemed genuinely sincere.

I went to the top deck to meet the others. Pietro was a well-built guy from Rhodes, Greece, who owned a watch shop. Stergiani was a pretty and slight young woman, also from Greece, with light-brown hair and blue eyes, aged thirty-one but looking ten years younger. We sat together on the deckchairs drifting downriver, village life extending to the riverbank languidly passing by.

"Have you ever drunk ayahuasca?" I asked Stergiani.

"No."

"Ever tried *any* kind of psychedelic?"

"Nope."

"You know what's in store tonight, right?"

"Yep. Well, kind of . . ."

What compelled her to travel all this way alone from Europe into the jungle to drink a powerful psychoactive brew that would blast her into an alternate state of consciousness with people she didn't know? That was the kind of thing you expect from young adventure-hungry men but not her—she was so demure, right down to her modest wispy dress covered with tiny flowers. She hadn't the faintest hint of the unconventional about her.

"Stergiani?"

"Yes?"

"What does your name mean?"

It was a long time before she answered. Looking at me, she said, very softly, "She who comes from the Earth."

I didn't speak for a while, letting images settle. From the Earth, I mused. Then spoke the words out loud. "She who comes from the Earth. Nice . . ."

I was in a dream. Better than a dream. We sat in silence, watching the view change as we sailed on and on to who knew where. I felt connected to Stergiani as if we'd known each other for years, yet we had only just met. I don't have sisters, but with this newfound emotional thread, I felt what it might be like to have a sister with whom I was very close.

Getting up to stretch my legs, I was drawn to the sound of talking. A group had gathered around a tall, slim, gray-haired man with a crew cut in his early sixties. It was Eddie—the ship's pizzazz, an American and a bona-fide one-of-a-kind, full of vitality and warmth. A freelance political consultant to a number of regimes in South America, he had worked for five different governments and was now contracted to work in Argentina. He had a wealthy, beautiful Argentinean wife. His charisma was alluring—so easy to listen to. Over the course of the trip, he held court, regaling us with stories. A very clever guy, always smiling. Fluent in Spanish, he translated for Andreas and some of his special Peruvian guests.

On the bus to the boat, I had become friendly with a young Californian, Josh. He exemplified the affable, laid-back West Coast stereotype. No hostility, so easy to get along with. Tall, well built, and with a shaggy mane of hair, he inspired confidence.

Then there was Robert—an accomplished heart surgeon for the previous eighteen years. Married, with three children, hailing from Norway. A classic Scandinavian, pale and blond, fine featured and boyish, with a strong jaw and blue eyes. Six feet five with broad shoulders. His hair was parted on one side, the epitome of conservative respectability. He had followed a straight line from school to medical school to the rarefied atmosphere of the higher echelons of the medical world— no detours. Yet, his clothes looked like they came from a local budget department store, plain and rather drab. Every day he dressed the same way: functional shorts, pastel-colored polo shirt, and sensible shoes. His voice was one of the softest and gentlest I had ever heard, giving the impression that he'd never resorted to any form of aggression in his life. A winner of life's golden ticket? Not quite. It was inevitable that some of his patients would not survive his surgery, and I'm sure his humility was partly attributable to this grim reality. A few days into the trip, he showed me a picture he carried in his wallet of his severely autistic eleven-year-old daughter. She was so disabled she was permanently confined to a baby carriage. He explained how unusual the photo was: he had managed to catch his daughter in a rare instance of actually looking into the camera. For almost her entire life, she avoided all eye contact with others, even her parents and brothers. When I asked him what his motivation was for coming on the voyage, he said, "To increase my compassion." He had an ethereal quality, aloof to the banality of everyday life. To describe him as deep would be a substantial understatement.

After a day sailing, the ship pulled close to the riverbank and moored. Andreas's team began preparations ashore for that night's ceremony. He had given us an indispensable list of items to take into the jungle at night. My patrol backpack had served me well up till now. Inside were water, a head-sized mosquito net, two types of industrial-strength insect repellent, two lock knives, a tiny waterproof survival kit, waterproof notepad and pencil, jungle/desert hat, a jacket, and two small Maglite torches with spare batteries.

Panos and I waited in our room until it was time to go ashore. I peeked out of our cabin's porthole. It appeared that the boat had been moored along a stretch of riverbank with no apparent purpose, as if Andreas had randomly picked a place in the jungle and said, "Here will do fine."

Killing time, Panos let me try on his beekeeper's hat, which he wore during ceremonies. It looked outlandish with its draped netting, but it was a practical choice for keeping mosquitoes off. Then we just lay on our beds staring at the ceiling in silence, waiting to be called to disembark from the boat deck.

At six thirty Rebecca knocked on our door and told us that it was time to go. The perfect summoner—a smoking hot Italian therapist, with long, dark curly hair and huge wide brown eyes. She peeked around our cabin door, delivering the inevitable invitation with poise. "Gentlemen, please make your way to the lower deck where we will board the canoe that will take us to land. Andreas is ready for you now to join the ceremony. The Mythic Voyage is going ashore." She closed the door quietly. Panos and I sprang up and grabbed our stuff. *This is it!*

15

The Gift of Ego Death

Force is temporary, consumes energy, moves from one location to another. Power is self-sustaining, permanent, stationery and invincible.

DAVID R. HAWKINS

We boarded the large motorized canoe that would take us all to where the riverbank met the jungle. The moon shone overhead, the water reflecting its brilliance like a mirror. The air temperature was a comfortable 75°F. Ten minutes later the boatman killed the motor, and the canoe began to drift toward the riverbank. Waiting on shore to greet us was Alfredo, who prepared the ayahuasca, and his crew of four men, who had already cleared a space in the jungle for the ceremony and would act as a safety team.

We stepped ashore. Torches flicked on, and everyone trod off in single file into the jungle, each person walking quickly and staying close to the person in front. No one wanted to get left behind or stray off the freshly beaten path. We came to the clearing. A quick flick of the torch revealed it to be about twenty meters wide. Standing in the middle were eight tiny Shipibo women. None of these medicine or holy women was taller than five feet and most appeared to be quite old. None flinched as our torchlights passed over their faces, their eyes shining brightly in the swathes of light.

Torchlight was the only light. Insects buzzing, and occasional whispers from group members were the only sounds apart from the gentle footfall of people as they moved around, choosing a place to sit. Twenty thin mattresses had been laid out around the edge of the clearing. The Shipibo shamanas—all trained ayahuasqueros—sat in a row in the middle. César, an elderly man with a wide, beatific smile— the Shipibo master ayahuasquero—was seated on the ground at one end of the line of women. He nodded a welcome to each of us as we settled in.

The mood was somber. We all attended to our own needs, making ourselves comfortable as best we could, aware of the implications of where we were and what we were about to do. Most checked to ensure their torch, water, and other comfort items were close to hand.

Andreas called us all to rise from our mattresses and move toward the middle of the clearing and form a circle. He said "Argonauts . . . happiness is a choice! And know this: it's also a skill, and with *intention* you can commit to making that choice and learning that skill."

He instructed us to face north and hold our arms up toward the sky with hands outstretched. He began an incantation, his voice booming into the darkness: "To the eagle of the north, soar above us. Look out for us and guide us as we journey inside."

He shuffled his bulk a quarter to the left, and we followed suit. "To the hummingbirds in the west, fly near and protect us, let your wings beat softly over us as we make this journey inside to peace."

We turned south. "To the spirit of the Anaconda, encircle us with your protective strength as we seek love from the Divine Mother of the forest."

Facing east. "To the spirit of the jaguar, give us your courage, your agility as we seek a connection to you and the spirit of the forest and of the Earth and the mighty river."

Turning for the last time back to the center of the clearing, we lowered our arms, completing the calling in of the directions with a loud *ho*. This ritual would start the ceremony each night.

César began to sing very softly. Andreas called out names in groups of four, and we crept forward to receive a cup from one of the female ayahuasqueros. Each person stoically drank the foul-tasting brew, a few shuddered in disgust as the thick brown gloop made its way from mouth to throat to stomach. We crept back to our mattresses and prepared to journey. Andreas admonished us to remain sitting upright for the next twenty minutes to ensure the ayahuasca sank deep into our stomachs. César stopped singing, and we sat in silence, waiting for the brew to take effect.

Out of nowhere a long swathe of light snaked into my peripheral vision. OK, here we go . . . Within minutes phantasmagorical visions erupted volcanically in cataclysmic sensory overload. I watched multi-colored geometrical shapes morph into organic sentient forms. As the visions came on in full force, I steadied myself. *You're grounded, you are sane.* Despite the attempt to self-soothe, the sensations escalated to the completely otherworldly.

The eight tiny Shipibo women singing icaros were unbelievable! Their voices harmonized beautifully in layer upon layer of exquisite choral vibration. Each of them was singing an entirely different song, but it was woven into an aural tapestry, a giant sound-shawl gently laid over us. Alien, yet soothing. Pure South American genius.

The singing was the cue for us to lie down flat on our mats. A few people had already started purging into their buckets. I glanced up at the sky and the jungle canopy above. Wow! I could only see a chunk of sky filling one-third of my visual field. The rest was a mass of dark foliage. The jungle was dancing! This was my first session outdoors, and everywhere the branches, shrubs, and vines were bathed in neon light and were in motion in a primordial dance. Through the dancing canopy, stars were shining like I'd never seen light shine before. Luminescence from a thousand fireflies flickered on and off. Seeing them burst here and there, flashing one second, dark the next, it seemed

Peter Pan's Tinkerbell and her friends had come to visit. I extended my arms trying to grab them, like a child reaching for bubbles. Then I lay still, and they landed on my outstretched forearms, lights flickering on and off in concert. This couldn't be happening! It was too magical!

The visual fireworks began to settle down, and I focused on my intention: show me how to trust. Overwhelmingly the thoughts were of my friend JJ. Over the next hour there wasn't a minute that went by when I didn't think of him. Here was that sense of the divine once again. I was feeling interconnected to everything, sensing how life on Earth was about *us,* the collective, not the individual. It's our separation that's causing our dis-ease and war. We are connected! My sense of ego diminished to something infinitesimally insignificant—to practically nothing—and it felt so good. For the first time in my life, I actually felt sensations emanating from my heart—emotions literally becoming heartfelt. Much of this energy was directed toward JJ. I sensed the pain from the catastrophe he had suffered in a way that was far more than empathy. *JJ, I feel you—all the way from the Amazon. My God, our God, dear God, I feel you in my soul, brother.* I felt comparable to a disciple and sensed that JJ was a true holy man. These were the extraordinarily peculiar thoughts that looped over and over for an hour. I got a sense that JJ had been born before and had been revered. It sounds insane, of course, but if you met him, you would know this was not an entirely insane thought.

My hands moved involuntarily, forming into a prayer position. An energy was controlling the actual physical position of my hands, so much so that when my hands moved away from one another, within a minute they mysteriously drew back together again in the prayer position, fingertips extended, touching lightly. Why did this always happen? I'm *not* religious but had an overwhelming sense that ayahuasca was teaching me something. JJ is a schoolteacher. I thought that he should come to the Amazon and drink. It was such a natural fit: the plant teacher and the schoolteacher. Together a formidable force for good. *JJ come to the Amazon and drink ayahuasca. I recommend it 100 percent. I recommend it 1,000 percent.* How ridiculous does that sound? But the same thought spilled over and over and over. *I recommend it 1,000 percent.* The words refused to go away.

The reverie was disturbed by queer noises coming from the people lying nearby. Until now everyone had remained disciplined and quiet. Occasionally, someone called out for Andreas, and he strode into the middle of the circle, his huge bulk silhouetted against ambient light from the moon and asked, "Who called me?"

When the person identified him- or herself, he went over and solved the problem. During the briefing on the ship, Andreas had told us that if someone appeared to be troubled or in need of assistance, we were to ignore them. He and his team would be on hand immediately to lend any assistance. He asked us to be selfish, to focus only on ourselves, to pay attention only to our intention. Hard as it might be, if someone needed assistance, we should not concern ourselves or take action—no matter how anguished the person seemed to be. "Do not help anyone!" he had explicitly commanded. Taking that instruction to heart had amplified the anticipation of what was to come.

But now exceptionally unusual noises were coming from a woman lying a few mattresses away. She was making a weird *ahhh* sound, more than a sigh, lasting as it did for five to ten seconds at a time. It started at a low pitch and rose higher and higher, or sometimes the reverse. Initially, rather than a woman in ecstasy, it sounded eerie. But it developed into much more than that—as if she were encountering an entity that possessed majesty so astounding that she was awed to a state where mere words were useless to express its magnificence. It was unnerving, the feeling you'd get from a wolf howling in the wild. She uttered occasional gasps of wonder, although she sounded simultaneously fearful and humbled in her rapture. At times it seemed as if she were on the cusp of either a scream or an uncontrollable laugh. I'd never heard anything like it. The noise must have been involuntary, because Andreas had instructed us to remain silent throughout the ceremony unless we needed his assistance. But as the ceremonies unfolded over the coming nights, this woman continued to make the same sounds.

In between my own intermittent gasps of wonder, introspection reigned. Understanding the significance of being able to detach my *self* from the ego was as insightful as learning the magnitude of the golden rule as a child. If only I could have parked my ego before now. It was infuriating that the solution to much of life's angst had always been hidden in plain sight if only the veil could have been lifted. The fights I could have sidestepped, the conflicts and squabbles, the overwhelming enormity of self-inflicted suffering that could have been avoided didn't bear thinking about. And with new comprehension I realized that it is entirely possible to cruise through life, from birth to death, and never even get out of the third gear of consciousness: asleep, awake, occasionally drunk. Repeat for eighty years. Die. There are men I know who *will* do this, of that there is no doubt. The unholy triumvirate of laws, beliefs, and culture will tragically exclude them from the psychedelic experience. A psychedelic encounter for many men would be like food to an anorexic—what could nourish them is denied, and denied by their own volition.

When the ceremony ended I lay there for a couple of minutes and watched the scene unfold as people rose up, shook themselves out of their introspection, and began talking. Robert, the heart surgeon, was near the foot of my mattress with Andreas, and I watched them embrace, two giants hugging. They held each other for a long while, an intimate moment. Andreas whispered in Robert's ear. He listened intently for what seemed like an eternity, then slowly nodded and embraced Andreas again, only this time they placed their hands on each other's upper arms and stared at each other in deep affection. Then they parted. I smiled, noticing a queue had formed behind Robert of other people who also wanted to thank Andreas. He asked us to thank César and the shamanas. We all clapped appreciatively, and they smiled rather shyly and nodded their heads in acknowledgment.

Back on board the ship, there was a celebratory atmosphere. Everyone seemed relieved that they'd gotten through the ceremony and were safe, sanity intact. Everyone I talked to was still very much feeling the aftereffects of the brew. People laughed, hugged, and kissed, inquiring, "So, how was it for you?"

I sat up on the top deck and shared a cigarette with Josh and Julian, the two young Americans. We were still feeling spaced out and woozy. I was thirsty and went to the dining room to grab a fruit juice. Glancing through the dining-room window, I saw Andreas sitting at the head of the long dining table on a high-backed chair reminiscent of a throne. He held a huge staff in his hand—a silent monarch. Two Australians—Phil and Trey—flanked him, sitting on each side, eyes closed, perhaps meditating. It was comically theatrical. I crashed into the room, breaking their trance. Andreas looked over, unfazed.

"Alex, how are you?" he asked, smiling warmly.

"Feeling supergood!" I gushed.

I got the juice, we said good night, and I trotted off to my cabin. Panos was still not back, and so I went over to the full-length mirror and stared at my reflection. My pupils were dilated. The beard—my first—longer than ever. Stripped to the waist, I could see ribs poking through. A pendulous crystal wrapped in a cross-section of ayahuasca vine hung on a leather cord around my neck. A castaway stared back at me—a grown-up Lord of the Flies survivor.

Panos returned, and we greeted each other like old friends. He looked deeply vulnerable as he described how he had developed what he referred to as a dark energy, a shadow, in his stomach area. He even had a specific name for this darkness—an Erebus, a kind of entity living in him. One of the reasons he had come on this trip was to try to manage his relationship with this Erebus. I surmised that Erebus were common to his part of Europe, a kind of ghoul that took up residence in certain unlucky people. He asked earnestly, "Do you have the same kind of thing where you come from?"

"I really don't think so."

Every night when he went to bed, he would liberally sprinkle Agua de Florida around him and tap his stomach with an eagle feather. While waiting to join the group back in Iquitos, he'd purchased the enormous feather, which was two feet long and six inches at its widest. He loved it, so much so that, before going to sleep each night, he gently waved it up and down, tapping the tip of the feather on his midriff, where the Erebus resided, furnishing himself the comfort he needed. The Agua de Florida is a sweet perfume often used by shamans and ayahuasqueros in ceremony to cleanse a person or environment of dark energy. It made our room stink.

Now, with this story of the Erebus, I understood that ritual—and that Panos was very superstitious. Sweet and gentle but plagued with doubts and conflicts exacerbated not only by his inability to see without glasses—to see things as they really are—but also by archaic beliefs about energies that could only be managed with rituals and potions. Then again, the shamans believed in and did the same thing. At the quantum level who really knows exactly what is happening?

In all the time we shared a room, Panos never once inquired about my life outside the Mythic Voyage: where I came from, who I was, if I had a family. I think he just enjoyed using his imagination.

I lay down and began to think about the war and the unorthodox possibility of how ayahuasca could help military men *prepare* for war *and heal* from war. If we could give modern combatants a sense of the possibility of an afterlife, as I had had with my very first experience with DMT, based on their own direct mystical experience and not something that was merely taught or dependent on faith, then this had to be worth exploring and a potential source of comfort. I lay there thinking that so much pain is endured by emotionally wounded troops. On returning to the US, more troops were committing suicide each year than were actually killed in Afghanistan. There are many men I know who have returned from serving in Iraq and Afghanistan who have suffered greatly, who are, at the very least, disillusioned. A friend of mine has serious post-traumatic stress disorder, is addicted to nicotine, and has been prescribed strong antidepressant medication for the last three years. Veterans like these are denied legal access to natural substances that can induce mystical states. Many feel misunderstood. Some go rogue and postal. Suicides are rife. Everyone loses. Surely, if a natural psychedelic could inspire me with such renewed optimism and faith in the value of life, then it could conceivably be of benefit to other veterans, too.

A totally unexpected gateway had opened in me to compassion, empathy, and a sense of everlasting life after death. The time for being culturally nudged into the seemingly blunt binary choice of being a religious believer or an atheist was over. This was a new alternative: spiritual. A new third way.

I drifted off to sleep feeling a genuine sense of forgiveness for my father and stepfathers. Once and for all, I had to just let that shit go.

16

How to Get Lost

The next morning, I traipsed over to the dining room. Breakfast was eggs, melon, guava juice, and bread. Conversation around the table was lively and convivial; people were invigorated by their experience the night before. After breakfast most people gathered on the upper deck to enjoy the sunshine and the view. We were now so remote from any-where that we hardly ever saw another boat—perhaps one a day. It was heartwarming to see the Shipibo ayahuasqeros interact with each other on the ship. They smiled constantly and wore intricately embroidered clothes and blankets during daylight hours. They were pleasantly plump and unquestionably happy. I had yet to see any one of them frown.

Andreas announced that throughout the day he would be holding one-to-one consultations on a first-come, first-served basis. Everybody scrambled like schoolchildren to get their names to the top of the list. He was enigmatic, and there was no denying the influence he had over many of the voyagers. I was intrigued and put my name on the list. The consultations started immediately, lasted all day, and he didn't take a single break. When it was my turn, I headed off to the library where they took place. He reclined in a grand red velvet armchair, his enor-mous bulk spilling out, like cake in a baking tray. "Come in. Welcome. Please take a seat!" His voice was deep and resonant, like Orson Welles with a Greek accent. His head was bald and shining, his black goatee neatly trimmed. He patted his face and head with a handkerchief to wipe away the perspiration.

I took a seat opposite. "Thank you. I'm not really sure where to start." It felt as if he was here to deliver an assessment, and I felt like a young boy about to be appraised by a headmaster. We made some small talk about the previous night's ceremony, and he asked me to forgive him for the insects and mosquitoes. A strange thing to say considering there wasn't anything he could have done about them. The chitchat didn't last long, and soon we got to the main course.

"Andreas, I've come here on this amazing journey, and I genuinely feel grateful to be surrounded by so many friendly people. But I do have one thing on my mind . . ." I stumbled, not really knowing how to articulate what I was feeling.

"Yes?" he prodded me.

"About a month ago I was in Afghanistan, in Helmand . . ."

Silence. He looked utterly unimpressed, his face a mask of ambivalence. If anything, his expression conveyed boredom. I must have been about the 120th person to get "the big thing" off his chest during a private consultation over the various voyages. His body language said, "So you think *that's* a big deal, do you big shot? Get over yourself. What's your point?" What he actually said was, "So what?" He nodded, waiting for a response.

When I didn't respond he pressed on. "So what?" He shrugged, fixing his gaze. "Was it heavy duty?"

More silence as we both considered what to say next. I still didn't speak.

"You know, Alex, you can say anything you want. Don't worry." His eyes remained intently on mine. It was intimidating. Nonetheless, I found my voice.

"Overall, it was bad. Nad Ali, where I was, is a violent and dangerous place. We were surrounded by gunfire and explosions all the time. One of my best friends was very badly wounded. I heard the bomb explode. It was terrible. It killed three men and injured several more." I paused, concerned I was rambling. "And I'm afraid to talk about it with anyone here on the boat because of the way it might make them feel. I don't want to bring anyone down because each person has invested so much into this trip."

More silence, as Andreas considered his response. He was quiet for a long, long time. Then finally, he spoke, his eyes boring into mine. "Alex, my brother, it is OK for you to talk about the war with anyone you want—and whenever you want—as long as you talk about it with beauty."

He let the words sink in momentarily before continuing. "Let me tell you something. The reason there is so much pain and suffering and war in the world is because humanity is going through a rapidly accelerated pace of change. The pain and suffering we witness all over the world is a direct consequence of this accelerated change. Please understand this. You *must* realize this."

He stopped talking. I didn't respond. I really didn't know how. Once he was satisfied that his unorthodox view had seeded, he continued, his eyes never leaving mine. "And, let me tell you something else that I know is real. The human race is mutating. We are mutating from *Homo sapiens* into beings of light, into what I call *Homo luminous*. We are evolving into self-programming beings of choice. This is the path that the human race is on. *This* is our destiny."

We spoke for a few more minutes before I said, "I have one more question. When I drink ayahuasca, I get a massively diminished sense of ego, and it's liberating, and yet when I'm back in England, I need an ego to lead a team, to compete and win. So my question is, how do you know when your ego is balanced and healthy?"

"It is perfectly fine for us all to have a sense of ego," he replied, "and we should befriend our egos because the ego comes from a pure source. There are two core drivers in nature—the need to survive and procreate. And in order to survive, you need to compete. And *that* requires ego. Here in the Amazon a young sapling on the forest floor will push its way to the top of the canopy to survive to be close to the light. But we should only compete *up to a point,* until survival is assured. *This* is the mistake that much of mankind makes because there is now an over-abundance of competitiveness. Symbiosis is the answer; cooperation is the key."

He took a breath and went on. "Secondly, we needed to procreate, to seek out mates. For this, we also need an ego. So let's not be naïve about these two fundamental drivers; to be selfish at times is natural. So I try to wear my ego lightly. I even have a name for him—I call him Larry."

He glanced to his left shoulder, as if his ego were perched there like a parrot. Grinning, he said, "How you doin', Larry?"

He stopped smiling, took a slow breath, and looked back at me intently. "And be careful what beliefs you choose. Beliefs are the source of all emotional suffering. We need concrete beliefs—that the floor will be solid when we decide to place our feet upon it. This is a belief that clearly serves us. But if a belief does not serve us, we must ask if the belief is really true or not. You should only accept beliefs that serve *you*," he stressed. "If you trust your intention to be happy, it will always lead toward the light. Trust your heart and you will not need moral rules."

As I rose to leave, he held out his arms as a signal to embrace. He gave me a bear hug, and it was slightly ridiculous—he was so huge that my arms failed to wrap very far around him. There was a two-foot gap between my hands as my arms extended around his back. Emotionally, it was another story. I felt a lump in my throat.

"Thank you. This has been a special conversation."

He smiled as I left. I was thinking about his words about the war. He'd provided me an intriguing new angle when talking about it—to do so within a larger context of hope and beauty, without denying its darker side. I knew I could do that, and I was grateful.

Beliefs. Would the world be a better place if there were no religions? Could we be spiritual without being dogmatically religious? Catholicism appeared now to be a significantly fear-based belief system, as were other global religious and faith-based systems. In Afghanistan many of the women were living appallingly bleak and wretched lives based on many of the Islamic beliefs they inherited. Men were offering up their lives as suicide bombers as a consequence of fundamentalism. I was becoming convinced that at a very deep level our fears, and fear-based emotions, were significantly impeding the development of humanity.

The next ceremony was dark. The crew had used machetes to clear a circular ceremony space on a small island. The mosquitoes were especially thick—a real infestation. Each insect that flew into my headspace felt like a minute hostile alien invader. Tonight I felt considerable unease. At the beginning of the ceremony, it felt like a black tentacled entity was creeping malignantly through my head, a bad primal energy. Shadowy spectral images loomed. I couldn't even remember the intention I had set for the ceremony; whatever it had been was obliterated by a pervasive sense of wickedness. Lying still and silent became a herculean task, and I continually jerked and twitched.

Others were purging, making painful groans and terrible gasps as they fought to regain their breath after exhausting bouts of sickness. Yet no one asked for help. The cacophony of pain and discomfort sounded horrific, each person struggling valiantly to stick with his or her intention. The combined simultaneous retching of both men and women rang out, sounding like the wildest of animals. Take the guttural bass of a tiger's snarl, melded with the trilling shriek of an elephant, then add in something indescribably alien. The ungodly acoustic accessory was the bucket. Swill the sound of each person's suffering around in their puke bucket and there you have it—something approximating the most horrible sci-fi soundtrack. Even the icaros sounded mournful. César and the eight Shipibo shamanas were singing, but their songs tonight were high-pitched wails. It felt like the clearing in the jungle had become some kind of a battlefield on which wounded souls cried out pitifully for help. What the hell was happening here? People sounded as if they were not just dying but actually undergoing a metamorphic shift, transforming from one wretched creature into another. The unpredictability of this trip was becoming eye-poppingly surreal.

Goading, enfeebling thoughts persisted. *You are weak.* Images of me going down with heat exhaustion and cramps in Afghanistan played over and over. Anxiety encroached like a swarming pestilence. My God, how the hell was this experience helping me, or any of us?

Andreas sat presiding in his chair, witnessing the collective anguish and doing precisely nothing. Corpulent, bald, and despicably silent, his only movement was to occasionally swab his sweating brow and face with the handkerchief he held in one hand. In the other, he grasped his ornate staff. He could hear and sense all this suffering. Why was he not helping us, or using his own energy to shift ours? Isn't that what a shaman is supposed to do? I began to convince myself that he had a ruthlessly opaque objective, and we were the unwitting victims. But there was no reaction from him or from any of the ayahuasqueros. What was his dreadful intention? Did he have a plan? Must we face our inner demons? He had continually encouraged us to "go deep," but deep into what, exactly?

Perhaps something truly horrible happened here on this island. Badness oozed, and it felt beyond eerie—at times even grotesque. It was with enormous relief when César and Andreas brought the ceremony to a close. Perhaps this was a lesson: there is no avoiding the duality that exists in the world. Irrefutably, good and evil exist; only our choices determine which path we will take. So be wise and choose carefully.

I was lying next to Eddie, and we began to discuss the ceremony. It had been just as unpleasant for him. As we got up he told me he had spent much of his time immersed in critical thought. In a low voice, almost a whisper so he'd not disturb the others, he began to explain his theory of why certain regimes in certain countries manipulate populations the way they do. Ordinarily, I enjoyed listening to him but not then. I was anxious and wanted nothing more than to return to the ship—away from the insects and the aura of malevolence. Eddie was deep into a diatribe, one based on experience, no doubt, since he advised many a government. As if sensing my mood, he explained, "You see, what manipulative regimes do to control people is . . ." I interrupted him.

"Sincerely," I said, looking directly at him so that he would know I was serious, "I already know what manipulative regimes do."

He put his hand on my shoulder and gently squeezed. "Sorry. Of course you do. Of course you do."

"I had a pretty rough ride tonight, and right now, I'd like to move away from the dark."

Josh, the young Californian, came over, his presence instantly lightening the mood. "Oh, man, that was intense!" he said, the whites of his eyes comically wide and bright in the darkness. Clearly, he had just been through his own ordeal. For some reason, he'd chosen to wear only a vest through the entire session, so his arms and shoulders were covered with swatches of red welts, although he didn't appear to notice. When I pointed them out, he just looked at his ravaged insect bitten skin and shrugged.

We were ready to leave and flicked on our torches to check that no kit had been left behind. Evidently, Eddie was still in critical-thought mode. As we walked single file along the jungle path back toward the boat, he said, "You know, I've been thinking . . . And you know what? This here—right now—what we've been experiencing on the Mythic Voyage with Andreas at the helm, you know what this is? It's a cult. *That's* what this is."

Alarm swept through me, the proclamation a double gut punch of betrayal. Right there and then, in that three-second moment, Eddie ruined everything. All the doubts about Andreas came flooding back, and any trust I'd had was now burst like a punctured balloon. Memories of the events of this voyage flooded back. He was right! Jesus Christ! How could I have been so naïve? I've been fucking *played* here. Andreas had drawn me into a goddamned cult!

Emotional pain blasted through me. The shame of being duped, trust violated, upset for having sleepwalked into a situation in which my vulnerability had been manipulated. Andreas was enormously charismatic, in some ways autocratic, and if I was honest, he sometimes seemed a little unhinged.

Cult. Cult. Cult. The words seared. My brow furrowed into an involuntary frown. You complete dick, I thought. How the fuck could you let yourself become so exposed? Only the weakest get duped like this, and now you've blundered out here, trapped in the middle of nowhere with a madman holding all the cards! My mind raced as we all clambered into the canoe and headed back to the riverboat.

Andreas sat directly opposite me in the canoe, less than three feet away, our knees practically touching. He was staring at me and smiling. Well, that's just great. It took enormous self-control to stop myself from actually groaning out loud that he was sitting so near while I was feeling so mistrustful. My lips were tight, face frozen in a frown. I tried to act casually, but it was useless. I was utterly on edge. Still hallucinating slightly (just what I didn't need), I sensed that Andreas knew *exactly* what I was thinking. *He's reading my mind!* I thought over and over. *He knows I know.* Then he looked right at me, leaned forward conspiratorially, and almost silently mouthed the words that I had to strain to hear. "*Homo luminous*, Alex," he said, smiling, nodding gently and pointing to his heart. "*Homo luminous.*"

I fought the temptation to lip-sync, "You're fucking *insane!*" but censored myself, literally forcing my body language to be passive and neutral, although my mind was the exact opposite. Things had just gotten even more sinister. This is an existential truck smash, and now I just want to kill the bastard.

The crewmen pushed the canoe off the bank, and Andreas made an announcement, bellowing, "Argonauts! Tomorrow morning at nine o'clock precisely everything will become apparent. There will be a big revelation! You will all see!"

He stared directly at me, his gaze unrelenting. This must be an act of bravado on his part because he sensed my dizzying collapse in faith. His eyes continued to bore into mine as he said histronically, "Yes! A *very* big revelation. Everything will change at nine o'clock. Just wait!"

His declaration sounded dangerous now, more like a threat given what I now knew. A kind of psychic lava oozed, destroying all goodwill. The whole world felt as if it were crashing down. I now perceived Andreas as a serious threat—not just an emotional threat but a very real physical one. Thinking back to his introductory speech as we had gathered on the boat about to start our adventure, he had roared, "Argonauts! You are all now fucked. Because you are all now *mine!* We are going on a journey hundreds of miles from anywhere, and you must trust me and do what I say."

My trust turned to vapor and vanished. All I was sure of now was that I was God-knows-where in the jungle, confined to a riverboat with a bunch of strangers who called themselves argonauts and entirely adrift within myself.

17

Never Get Out of the Boat

Back on board the boat, my mind blared at DEFCON 1, manifesting as white noise panic turned up to ten. Concern amplified, with the realization that no one but Andreas knew about the safety of the ayahuasca. No one but him really knew how this batch was made or what was *in* it. The ceremony had been dreadful, so perhaps he was monkeying with the traditional recipe? The safe ingredients were the traditional natural ones—ayahuasca vine, chacruna leaves, and water. The Mythic Voyage website had extolled the benefits of other psychedelic compounds such as mescaline, which comes from peyote or San Pedro cacti.

The most troubling thought was that he might have added in datura—an extremely powerful psychotropic plant occasionally used by shamans in very tiny quantities. Its lethality is well known, as it can be fatal in high doses. It is notoriously unpredictable and difficult to measure a safe dose. Certainly not a compound to play around with. For centuries it had been used in parts of Europe and India as a poison. It has long been associated with witchcraft—one of its effects is to produce the sensation of flying. Sometimes users can't distinguish fantasy from reality, and it pushes them over the edge into delirium. It was not uncommon in Amazonian regions for small doses to be used as an additive to ayahuasca. With my distrust heightened for both Andreas and the ayahuasca, I thought about the book by Carlos Castaneda that I had read while holed up in the hotel in Iquitos waiting to join the voyage. Castaneda sold millions of books worldwide, and his is arguably the most recognized name among the pioneers of shamanic exploits. But what many people don't know is that he had been adversely affected by datura. Later in life, when living as a recluse in a walled compound in Los Angeles, accompanied only by his "witches"—apprentices and former anthropology students from when he taught at UCLA—he reminisced that he had suffered immense physical and psychological damage from datura as part of his shamanic initiation.

"If you're not paranoid, you're not contributing to the team." War wisdom still percolated up, the kind that doesn't help you in peacetime.

At breakfast I kept to myself, necked the food in six big gulps, and left the room. I needed to get a second opinion about the cult. The short-term plan was to find Robert. Then follow up with Eddie. If he insisted on making cult accusations, then he was going to have to justify himself. As I searched for Robert, thoughts spiraled off into dark corridors of paranoia. I wasn't on this journey to do datura or some other unknown potent substance. I was here to recover physically, mentally—to grow spiritually—not to be poisoned in some lame replication of the Jim Jones's Jonestown Kool-Aid massacre.

In November 1978, 913 American cult members, all of them devout followers of the charismatic leader and self-appointed minister Jim Jones, died in a commune called Jonestown in Guyana in the South American jungle. Jones was a fake faith healer from the Midwest, and his devout following of believers were ordered to drink cyanide-laced Kool-Aid in the largest ritual suicide in history. Hundreds of victims were children. This sickening waste of life was as incomprehensible as the bombings of schools by the Taliban. Repellent religious beliefs gone rotten.

Andreas had us all over a barrel, our vulnerability assured—and he knew it. We were deprived of sleep, on a restricted diet, had no contact with the outside world. Perhaps he had the intention of using psychotropic compounds to control our consciousness—the possibilities for manipulation were endless. I even spun out an *Apocalypse Now* scenario, with Andreas playing the role of the rogue and demented Colonel Kurtz. We were all doomed. As Martin Sheen had said in the movie, "Never get out of the boat. Absolutely goddamn right."

I couldn't find either Robert or Eddie before the time came to return to the dining room for Andreas's 9 a.m. revelation, and so with a heavy heart I joined the others. Unfathomably, the "big revelation" turned out to be some kind of absurdist theater, a bizarre piece of performance art. The dining-room table had been moved out of the way to create a large open space where Andreas could perform. He began by ranting for five minutes, stamping the floor with his feet, smacking his forehead violently with the palm of one hand, while shouting a string of words, including "Belief!" and "Trust!" I was mystified. Others looked embarrassed and uncomfortable, not knowing how to react. Surely this was a man in the midst of a mental breakdown. The performance was soon over—time to get out of there. I saw Eddie and seized my chance. This was no time to vacillate, so I marched straight up to him, looked him dead in the eye, and ordered, "You, me, my cabin—now!"

We sat down on opposite beds facing each other, and I began to rant, "Listen, last night when we left the ceremony, you said that you thought we were immersed in a cult. Where I come from that's a serious word— I'm sure it means the same where you're from. So don't tell me there's no fuckery afoot here! The last thing I want right now is another leader— I've had enough of them. One of the biggest problems we have is our addiction to leadership. I'm freaking out thinking we've been manipulated, that we're vulnerable—exposed—in the hands of a madman who plans to do who knows what with us while we're playing out here off the reservation, completely out in the middle of fucking nowhere!"

Eddie replied steadily and evenly. "OK, cool your jets—no need to start flipping tables. Look, you saw the guy's performance this morning, right? He's clearly losing his shit. Didn't that look to you like a man who's unhinged? The power's gone to his head! It's as clear as day that he is undergoing some kind of a mental breakdown."

Exactly. A breakdown! Fuck. What to do? I calmed down, searching for logic.

"It's not a cult. Surely. There's no real estate involved. None of us has given up our worldly possessions and renounced our families to go and live with him on a permanent basis. That's what cults do, right? We're not that stupid. We came here to have some kind of redemptive cathartic experience, didn't we? This is supposed to be a journey of discovery. Besides, many people have been here several times, so if he was going to do something dangerous, surely it would have been exposed by now on previous trips? Look at the following he has here—people love him! You and I both have every intention of returning to the normal world and resuming our lives, don't we?"

He agreed—a huge relief.

"OK, I'm sorry. Maybe I was being a little too provocative."

Perhaps Eddie had begun to have his own doubts and had been looking for others' opinions without expressly asking, or perhaps what he said about this being a cult had been just a throwaway line. I didn't know, but now he was getting my opinion with both barrels.

"The thing I'm most worried about," I said, "is what exactly is *in* the ayahuasca? Based on my experience it feels like ayahuasca to me. But I'm honestly concerned that Andreas may slip in something insidious—something experimentally toxic—as we get further and further away from civilization. He may want us to get more out of it for reasons that are unknown to us. And I don't want to have a really bad trip and come out of the experience with some long-term psychological damage. I've got real-world responsibilities, as do you. I'm not about to piss all that away. I didn't come here for that."

Eddie continued to pacify me, and I stopped flapping and came down from the ceiling. I spent the next hour listening to his head-spinning life story. Finally, I had to escape the cabin and get some fresh air. I also desperately sought out Robert in an effort to evoke some expeditionary solidarity. I found him on his own on the upper deck. "Robert, may I speak to you for a minute, please?"

"Of course, anytime." He motioned toward the empty chair next to him.

"How's things?"

"Oh, you know, just feeling . . ." He paused, rummaging for the right word. ". . . very, very quiet."

His voice was barely audible, and he had such an ethereal quality about him, so gentle—and he looked so pale. His introspection bordered on melancholy, and who on Earth could blame him? In that instant I vicariously felt the burden of responsibility that he carried. Not only did he have a severely autistic daughter, but every week he plunged, quite literally, into the hearts of men and women, applying surgical skills in do-or-die situations. Inevitably, some would not survive the surgery, so then he had the added burden of dealing with the deceased's distraught family, not to mention his own emotional upset. The responsibility must be immense, and I didn't envy him at all. *Of course* he was feeling quiet and reflective. He was entitled to. I felt guilty for disturbing him, yet still a little desperate to air my own concerns. I held back from my own agenda and instead reached out.

"You know, Robert, if you need to talk, I'm here for you. Whenever you want to talk."

He didn't respond. I couldn't read his expression, but as sincere as my offer had been, what comfort could I really offer him?

After a short period of silence, it was my turn to be provocative. "You know, I feel that, to some degree, we have both led extreme lives, although obviously in different ways."

His eyes darted to meet mine, alert at the use of the word *extreme*. He began to open up. "I live in a nice house," he said. "I have a loving wife and three children—all the material wealth and success a man needs. But I can't help thinking what else I could have done with my life. Since the age of eighteen, my life has been mapped out for me."

He was genuinely rueful, and I did my best to make him feel better without being patronizing. We agreed we were both on this trip on a quest for meaning and beauty that we could take back to our real-world lives. At the very least, we were here to enjoy novelty and strangeness, to stretch and grow. I reminded him that he, unlike many other people, had the freedom and opportunity to do things like this. Too many professions constrain people, shackling them in golden handcuffs, defining them, medicine being a prime example. He hadn't allowed himself to be totally boxed in. He wasn't just a surgeon. He was on his own quest. Most of us get so invested in our professions, they become a measure of our self-worth, and it confuses our real identities. He and I were each struggling to not let that happen.

Although he appeared to be listening, his attention was on the tattoo that covered my shoulder and upper arm. He studied it as I spoke. When I finished he didn't respond to anything I said. Instead, out of the blue he said, "Your tattoo is quite beautiful."

I was flattered. A British commando dagger was encircled by a laurel wreath, which itself was encircled by the flowing script "Royal Marines Commando." Notably, he'd moved the conversation away from his life's purpose. Accepting the cue, I jumped right in.

"Can I ask you something important?"

"Of course."

"Last night, Eddie said that the Mythic Voyage is a cult . . ."

I shut up and studied his face closely, watching for his reaction to the *C* word. "What do you think?"

His pale blue eyes met mine, and his brow furrowed. After some time he said emphatically, "It is not a cult." He shook his head with confidence and repeated, "It's not a cult."

His reasoning followed mine. There did, indeed, seem to be a cult of personality with Andreas. That was a given. He reasoned, "I don't agree with everything Andreas says. He can be annoying and he can be rude—he even admits that himself—but he's not running a cult. It's kind of culty, perhaps, but not a cult."

"OK," I said, as I had to Eddie, "but I'm still worried about what might be *in* the ayahuasca. You may have seen on his website that he has every intention of using mescaline at some point in this trip. And if he's intent on bringing mescaline into the ceremony as a sacrament, in much the way that the Native North Americans traditionally harvest it from a cactus, then I think we have a right to know, don't you?" I didn't give him an opening and pressed on. "I don't want mescaline mixed in. Who knows what the result would be if you mixed those two hallucinogens. It could be dangerous. And I definitely don't want him adding datura! I know shamans here use it occasionally, but I think it's too much of a risk when we don't know the correct dosage. As a medical man, I'm sure you can appreciate that."

"Don't worry," he assured me. "All we're drinking is ayahuasca. I trust Andreas. He'd tell us if it was anything else."

I thanked him and wandered away, brooding. I sat on deck, easing effortlessly into a daydream. The key element that I was struggling with deep down was 100 percent self-government—forever. Complete autonomy for the rest of my life. In the military, to a certain degree, they own you and you are complicit in the pact: *you can micromanage me and I'll take the macroexperiential benefits.* These benefits included, and were not limited to, free travel to wild and dangerous places, guaranteed adventure and excitement, the opportunity to make friends you can trust with your life, for life. The alliance of control within the corporate world is different. With that agreement you devote 70 percent of your alert problem-solving time to the company, and it, in turn, can grant you the wealth that helps contribute to a contented family. But I had had enough of both of these paradigms. I wanted to think for myself. The last thing I needed was another leader or any other element of control over my actions and time. I was becoming a free man; I could taste it. I just had to work through these last vestiges of resistance, which were like mist to a sailor who knows it will clear when the sun reaches its zenith.

Andreas had reinforced that we are all empowered to consciously choose our own beliefs. So I followed his advice. Did this cult belief feel good? No. Then reject it. Cut it down with the simple application of first world rational thought. I worked to annihilate the last remaining doubts. Providing Andreas didn't surreptitiously try to poison us, the likelihood was that I would get out of this place alive. I had to acknowledge his track record. People came back over and over again, endorsing him and the voyage. Even when the rest of us were swimming in the fog of ayahuasca, he always had his game on, lucid and on point. I had never once seen him pause for thought—his mind sharp and instant. I made an effort to ditch my paranoia right there and then. This entire episode had been a self-inflicted fear burden. Maybe the lesson here for me was trust. Hadn't that been one of my intentions in an earlier ceremony—to learn how to trust *completely?* Maybe this had been a test?

That became the thought I mulled over and over as we sailed on downstream. After a day or so of orchestrated mind manipulation, I reconvinced myself that I was a lucky bastard, ready for deep immersion into what friends at festivals referred to as "the fuck-about zone." It was playtime.

18

Question Authority, Trust Yourself

Nature loves courage.

Terence McKenna

As well as Orson Welles, Andreas, in fairness, was equally part Deepak Chopra and Eckhart Tolle. Winner of the world's most anarchic tour guide. I felt sheepish about my prior snap judgment. I could see him now as an enabler, guiding those in need out of the deadening constraints of pain, doubts, and self-imposed roles and rules.

You had to give him credit: he envisioned this entire voyage and ran it with an iron fist cloaked in a velvet glove. He liked weird and embraced it, just as I did. Besides, the guy had balls. A journey of this type was risky. Like Richard from La Kapok Center, he was a pioneer, a frontiersman, with an unshakable conviction for the sacramental potential of ayahuasca and other plant-based entheogens. He knew that since the beginning of time, humans have felt compelled to shift their state of consciousness, that we are both seekers of pleasure *and* mystery, that our curiosity propels us. The Afghans have their opium, and the Amazonians have ayahuasca. We shared the view that there was nothing wrong with most psychedelics as long as *you* remained their master. He had tapped into the zeitgeist that secular living, archaic belief-based religions, and rampant, unchecked capitalism are not sustainable or satisfying for millions of people. Aspects work, but there were gaping chasms of inadequacy. The growing global search for deeper spiritual meaning was an attempt to address this. He realized that on a fundamental level the philosophy of "he who dies with the most toys wins" doesn't even qualify as a bad joke and that the people of the Amazon had glimpsed the solution. When he kept his tendency toward megalomania in check, Andreas could be inspiring.

Here in the Amazon trust truly was the order of the day. In Afghanistan we had maps that were so detailed that every single mud hut and crumbling compound wall could be identified. We knew where we were to the nearest fifty meters. Contrast that with the Amazon. Here, I'd relinquished responsibility for navigating entirely and had no idea where I was to the nearest five hundred miles. A counterintuitive paradox: I was lost and had never felt safer.

I resolved to go into the ceremony that night with a clear and strong intention: "Show me an important truth."

During the day the Shipibo women gave us flower baths with a bucket of clear river water in which scented flowers had been steeped. We took turns on the upper deck, the women lightly scrubbing each person down from head to toe. It was wonderful, and the flower blossoms smelled heavenly.

In the afternoon the skipper moored the ship at a confluence where three channels joined. Some of the women squealed in delight as pink freshwater dolphins jumped in and out of the river, playfully circling the boat. Ben, Andreas's right-hand man, entertained us by performing backflips and somersaults off the bow into the river.

Ben was Andreas's lieutenant, assisting him on every Mythic Voyage. He had the feline quality of a muscular jungle cat. Thirty, supercharged with positivity, he stood over six feet tall and had shoulder-length blond hair and blue eyes, obviously in his prime. It was his job to recce and prep the jungle ceremony locations. He also ran some of the ceremonies and morning workshops. For the first few days, he'd been busy with his duties, so when I finally did get to spend some time with him, I realized he had the air of something extraordinary about him. He had grown up in Holland and so spoke with a Dutch accent and had lived in Los Angeles from the age of sixteen. He was a dedicated devotee to the Burning Man Fesitval—that iconic temporary community of free spirits and artists who convene in the Nevada desert every August. He had spent five years as a professional footballer and now was an accomplished artist and musician: he played the flute with beguiling beauty. He had a small land holding in Colombia where he grew crops and had traveled extensively throughout Central and South America earning a living as a snake hunter milking venom to make antivenoms for snakebites. He learned this trade from a master snake hunter, but that's another story. Much of his time over the past two years had been spent campaigning to free slaves in India and donating his art to civic projects that helped the freed slaves assimilate back into the world. So there you have it—a somewhat preposterous smorgasbord of good qualities. He grinned a lot, was always affable, and his integrity and openness, combined with his good looks, were no doubt why the women on board especially seemed drawn to him.

It grew dark—time for the ceremony. Ashore in the jungle we each took a cup of ayahuasca and settled in our places, waiting for the magic show to begin. Within ten minutes a single thought came crashing into my consciousness with a force that felt physical, beyond mere thought—a message delivered as a pulse of energy: "Have No Fear!"

Without subtlety or nuance, the words had individual power: *Have—No—Fear*. Where the hell did that come from? I had asked to be shown a truth but was this true? Considering all I'd put myself through with the whole cult meltdown, I doubted it. I feigned disinterest, shifting thoughts, but the words crashed into awareness again and again. It was becoming clear now that a portion of my brain/consciousness had been utterly dormant—waiting for the key to be turned. My ego, along with the fear paired with it, had been holding me back from revealing my true nature, and it had done so since early childhood.

At one point during the ceremony, I became aware of strange breezes; nothing like normal breezes, they seemed to defy physics. Probably some kind of meteorological phenomenon I'd never heard of. Each stream of air felt like it had a form, as thin as a pencil. One of them had a curious movement that started from apparently nowhere below my chin, flowed over my chin and the tip of my nose, and then continued upward between my eyes to my forehead. It was very weird. Almost as if someone were blowing on my face from chin to forehead with a straw. What was going *on*? A stream of air, no insects fluttering, it didn't seem natural; in fact, it felt supernatural, like a ghost might feel if it brushed against bare skin. I really didn't know what to make of it but let it continue to flow. Eventually it stopped, just as suddenly as it had begun.

Minutes later there was more strangeness. I moved my head to one side and felt the whole side of my face enter a cooler patch of air. Tilting my head back, the air was normal, warm again. I moved my head back into the cold patch—just to test it—still cold. I repeated this process several times to make sure it wasn't my imagination. Hot then cool, hot then cool. Whole chunks of air surrounding my body appeared to have different atmospheric properties. It was so perplexing.

The cacophony of a billion insects chirped, rasped, and buzzed. There was an opening in the jungle canopy to the moon and stars that funneled light directly into the center of the ceremonial space.

I began to shiver. The shamanas' icaros were powerful tonight, each of them singing different songs, melodies blending to make one gorgeous interwoven sound. Some of their voices were implausibly highly pitched, like cartoon characters digitally manipulated to sound almost frenzied. It would have been comical if it weren't so sensational. It is almost impossible to describe the effect of the icaros. Sound modulates consciousness; it plays with it, transforms it—as if the shamanas were conductors, orchestrating minds with tunes. Their voices crafted energy into sumptuously colored patterns, complex matrices of energy that revealed the core of reality. It was so obvious now how *everything* is made of energy. Their songs were the brushes of an energy palette, painting the invisible into the visible, sounds generating light.

One of the tiny shamanas crept over, sat cross-legged at my feet, and directed her song right at me, stretching her arms to the treetops, gently waving her hands aloft in reverence. I could feel the vibrations from her song physically reverberate through me. The shivering intensified, my body processing vibratory waves of pleasure. Fireflies floated over her, landing on her shoulders and head, some of them appeared to synchronize their twinkling—glittering like Christmas lights—in time with the rhythm of her song. It was mesmerizing.

The ayahuasca took me deeper. Looking up, I saw the full moon was centered within the canopy opening. Its radiance was of divine proportions—like a ten-million-candle spotlight beamed from a benevolent cosmos. The brilliance accentuated the surrounding darkness of the jungle. The drifting clouds morphed constantly into new shapes, each representing an expression of a comforting cosmic code. Unfathomably deep neon geometry flooded the blackness behind the moon and stars, spiraling to infinity. I was dumbfounded as beauty spilled from the dazzling vista, causing my jaw to slowly drop, slacker than a sail without wind. I glanced to my right, at Rebecca—she was exactly the same as me: eyes and mouth wide open, staring transfixed, bathed in wonder. I began to comprehend that ocean upon ocean of limitless creative potential poured endlessly from the heavens, that we are embedded in an energetic matrix of inexpressible concentrated beauty, that the very essence of existence is unconditional love.

This must be what it feels like to die, I thought, as my body vibrated and my consciousness seemed to merge with matter, beyond the boundaries of my physical self. Death is a process, not an end, and now I knew what it felt like to be immersed in that process, at least in part. As my body shivered and vibrated, I felt that in some inexplicable way I was ascending. This must be ascension of a kind. Or perhaps the heavens were descending. It was hard to tell. I sensed the ultimate connection, a oneness with the Great Mystery so powerful that I thought the surge of emotion and insight might short-circuit my nervous system. Either that, or I'd puke, roll over, and freak out, simply unable to cope. The potency—the avalanche of intelligence and information beaming its way like a laser beam—held me on a knife's edge between reverence and breakdown. The plants were teaching me that instead of knuckling down, working hard, and following the direction of leaders, we had to instead engage the application of limitless imagination. The lesson, even if I had the audacity to try to ignore it, was to ditch fear and *create* something.

Andreas approached. I lay on my back, and he knelt down next to me and laid his hand over my heart and whispered words of compassion in my ear. Beads of sweat, like translucent bubble wrap, dappled the top of his head, each one encapsulating its own tiny rainbow of colors. His face morphed wildly from a jester to a Mexican wrestler's mask, then into a series of rapid-fire demonic caricatures, each mask changing by the second. There was unmistakable humor behind the archetypes—a cosmic joke. The images contrasted with the kind and gentle words he spoke, and eventually I had to close my eyes to keep from being overwhelmed by the strangeness of the masks transforming his face.

The new "empathy" sense was back, like a kind of telepathy. I couldn't read anyone's thoughts—obviously—but I had an overpowering sense of how people nearby were feeling.

I didn't want this ceremony to end, but when it did I took my time packing up my stuff. As we made ready to leave, I saw one of the twins still sitting on her mattress, crying quietly. I went over. "Are you OK?" I asked, gently. I reached out and held her hand.

"It's *so* beautiful," she whispered between sobs. "So beautiful . . ."

Out of nowhere my head began to spin in a wave of nausea. I reached for a nearby bucket and purged heavily. Ben was close by and laughed at me. "It's a beautiful thing to do, isn't it?" he said, as I tried to regain some breath and composure. He went on. "It's like a portal to my higher self, my higher authentic self—the fully optimized one. Like a celestial promise—I break through a boundary and it feels like I've shed a layer, don't you think?" Then he concluded with, "And I hope you said thank you!"

My head was still gurgling in the bucket. He threw his head back laughing at my gasps, knowing full well I was in no state to respond.

We snaked in single file back down the path through the jungle to the river. I was at the back of the line and began to hear gasps of what sounded like joy and uproarious surprise. I quickened my pace to catch up and see what the commotion was about. As I approached the canoe, the sounds became louder. No mistaking it—something unexpected and very pleasing was occurring ahead. Once able to break free of the forest, I saw people standing on the shore looking up at the sky, groaning with pleasure. I followed their gaze. Above was the most unusual and sublime cloud formation I'd ever seen. Nestled against a jet black background, long, cylindrical cirrus clouds striped across the entire sky— there were hundreds of them, identically sized, shaped, and spaced. The sight was beyond epic. Every single cloud was exactly the same shape. Perfectly identical—even down to the regularity of the spacing between them. Between the clouds stars shone brilliantly, like backlit diamonds, so very, very bright that the river *itself* was alight, shining with their reflections.

We stood there on the riverbank for a long time, speechless. I had never seen stars shine and reflect in water before. It was like lights from a festival had been waterproofed, strung out, and submerged as far as the eye could see. Ben urged us to board the canoe. Once we were all aboard, the canoe drifted from the riverbank out into the huge expanse of the river, which must have been two miles wide. As we moved away from the land, the true awesomeness of the spectacle became even more apparent. The entire surface of the mighty river reflected the glittering stars in all their glory—the only sight I have ever seen that appeared to be of biblical proportions. It had a powerful emotional impact, genuinely otherworldly. As above, so below. If we had been entranced before, we were now breathless. All I could hear were people shouting, "Wow. Wow, *wow!*" Like a scene from a gigantically budgeted 3-D science-fiction movie—only much, much more impressive. To this Englishman, it was way beyond cinematic. More and more I was feeling that the Amazon is a gift—preposterously beautiful and enchanting. The river's majesty undeniable, equal companion to the jungle—its absolute and unmatched partner. The power here was palpable.

The canoe trip back to the ship took only ten minutes, but it was far and away the most memorable ride of my life. When you are floating on a small boat on a river that's at least more than a mile wide and the sky becomes everything in your field of view, especially when the black glassy river below exactly mirrors the sky above, it is possibly the closest terrestrial sensation to actually floating in space. Twenty sets of eyes gazed upward in mute astonishment. I didn't want to move my eyes away for a second more than necessary, but I was also desperate to glance again at my companions' faces. All of them were shaking their heads in wonder, almost everyone's mouth was agape in a literally jaw-dropping response. Everyone was quiet now, struck dumb with the original awe.

We got back to the riverboat and scrambled aboard, people taking a moment to hug one another. Some argonauts were wobbly on their feet and had difficulty transferring from boat to ship, so Ben stayed back to help them. I was last off and grasped his hand to steady me as I jumped aboard the larger vessel. As we said good night, I whispered in his ear, "You get a triple-A rating for tonight's ceremony and nature show. Man, that was truly amazing! Thank you!"

"Well, I've no idea what that means," he said. "But I'll take it, thanks all the same."

Of course this had nothing to do with a triple-A finance rating. Triple A had taken on an entirely different meaning for me during the ayahuasca ceremony. At its visionary peak, when the feelings were most intense and the singing from the Shipibo women was at its most exquisite, I had felt a symbol as a shaft of energy: AAA—Afghanistan-Ayahuasca-Amazon. The trinity that represented my recent life. Neat, clean, and true.

I went up to the top deck after dumping my kit in my cabin. As I climbed the stairs, I could see the usual suspects were already there: Sophie, Pietro, Anna. They were smoking cigarettes, but their faces were still agog in rapt amazement, their heads craned as far back as possible, mouths wide open.

"Look!" they said, as my head appeared through the opening from the lower deck. Jeez, what could possibly top the treat we'd just witnessed?

I climbed out on deck and looked up. The moon, utterly dazzling and easily twice its normal size, was encircled by several bands of colored lights that merged like a rainbow! I had never seen anything like it: the moon with colored rings! The stars surrounding the moon were all similarly encircled with a single band of bright white light. This could be what the sky on an alien planet might look like. So beautiful, so powerful—I simply had no idea that the moon could shine so brightly, like a laser beaming wisdom. We squinted and practically needed sunglasses to hold our gaze. It was as if all the atmospheric conditions that normally shield the moon had been lifted at last, a veil swept aside to reveal the *real* moon.

Pietro turned to me, smiled, offered me a cigarette. Very deliberately and slowly he said, "Alex, welcome . . . to the *full* moon. Welcome to 11,11,11. Welcome to the illumination."

I looked at my watch and checked the date. He was right! It was November 11, 2011. An exquisite synchronicity. I laughed and had to stop myself ranting like a bad impersonator from *Monty Python's Life of Brian*, "It's a sign! It's a sign—a celestial promise! All is Oneness. Everything is one, everything connected to the same single source! One love." I was shouting the words in my head.

In some small way that night, *we* had become illuminated. In some small, significant way, we had all been changed forever—a spark ignited. The time-bound symbol of 11.11.11 encapsulated a perfect moment; that right *here* right *now* with *these* people bathed in the light of *these* stars and *this* moon in *this* forest was the closest I was ever going to get to experiencing heaven on Earth. As above, so below—this *is* heaven on Earth.

The remnants of the jungle brew coursed through us. We stood staring, reduced to silence. What more was there to say?

19

Evil Exists, Confront It

I stumbled down to the cabin. Panos was lying on his bed muttering under his breath, eyes shut. He began to sing and chant softly to himself, engaging in his now-familiar ritual of tapping his midriff with his eagle feather.

The next morning, curious about his ritual, I asked, "You know the Erebus that lives inside of you, the darkness in your stomach?"

"Yes."

"You know . . . ," I said slowly, making sure he could see me looking at him, "it may not really be there . . . Have you thought about that? This could just be a belief, a superstition. Perhaps you could choose that it doesn't exist. Have you tried that? If you choose to disbelieve in it, you might find that the pain will go. Or you could try a doctor . . ."

He looked perplexed, no doubt thinking if only it could be that simple.

He wasn't the only person who believed an eagle feather had healing properties. Months later JJ told me that he and thirty wounded British soldiers and marines—many of them amputees—had been funded by a charity to visit the Grand Canyon. They had taken part in a North American Indian healing ceremony. A medicine man had gently tapped each man's injury with an eagle feather, explaining that traditionally this was how his ancestors had helped heal their warriors' wounds after a battle. The feather helped to carry the pain back to where the injury had occurred, leaving the wounded man free to go forward. JJ said that he had found the ritual extremely moving.

The morning after our incredible night, after breakfast, we gathered in the dining room for a workshop. Andreas kicked off the proceedings, roaring, "Good morning, argonauts! Welcome to another beautiful day of the voyage. I think we can all agree that last night was very special. Many of you, I know, plunged deep—felt connected. In some way many of you have evolved. So I'd like to invite you to speak about your experiences. Is there anything that you'd like to share with all of us?"

I was first to my feet. Ordinarily, I would be shy about being the first to step forward, but the message from last night still chimed like a tuning fork. Once on my feet, I said, "I felt I was sent a very precise message. I don't know where it came from, but it arrived very clearly, like a voice. The message was 'Have no fear.'"

Still inspired, on a roll, I continued. "And last night I realized that fear is just a motivator. And now I really feel like I don't have any unnecessary fear—and I am grateful. Someone once told me the letters F-E-A-R are an acronym meaning 'false expectations appearing real.' Now I believe it. Thanks."

I sat down, expecting contagious approval, people leaping up, parodying "I'm Spartacus," each person declaring boldly, "I *too* have no fear!" But the imagined crescendo of agreement wilted to an avalanche of apathy. No one responded. No cartwheels, no joy. It was clear that we were all on different odysseys. No one but Andreas knew I'd arrived from Afghanistan or had in any way been connected to the war. They had no way of knowing that the no-fear message had significance because I'd spent much of the previous year in a fearful state. Fearful an insurgent would lob a grenade that would roll into a tent. Fearful the chopper flying us between tasks would be blown out of the sky by an RPG. Fearful that when I stepped outside the fort, I would be blown up or shot. Fear that while checking a man's ID, he would detonate a suicide vest. No one apart from Andreas had any idea about any of this. The message that night had been only for me.

Yet there was the realization that I *was* freed from fear. I was safe, away from the war and more tours of duty. Another way of interpreting the message was, "Have no fear *anymore*." Irrespective of whether it was my subconscious or ayahuasca that sent the message—the messenger was irrelevant—I had had another epiphany and could move on.

Eddie stood up next. "Good morning, everyone. Last night I kept getting this incredibly warm feeling of brotherly love for Robert." He paused. "I could feel an undeniable physical sensation in my heart."

Others stood to follow suit, sharing their experiences. Some women had had a difficult time during the ceremony and were tearful as they recounted their stories. Then Panos stood to speak. "Yesterday, I had an encounter with an eagle. He flew nearby and settled on a branch nearest to me from the bank when we were moored. I felt connected to it. He wanted to communicate. It was beautiful. When I slept last night, I felt like I had *become* an eagle. I flew high enough to see everything! Everything is clearer now."

He sat down. The daytime eagle had been real enough. He had called me over, excitedly pointing it out on the branch on the riverbank. He still possessed his impressive eagle feather, and last night his "power animal" had shown up in his dream. I noticed for the first time that he was not wearing his glasses. For the rest of the voyage, he abandoned them.

As night fell I prepared my kit. The strangest ceremony yet was about to be unleashed.

Andreas suggested an intention that I might want to use that night. Instead of choosing one that made sense or was reassuring, he suggested that I ask ayahuasca to "Show me something that is not perfect."

Show me something that's *not* perfect? Really—why bother? What good could come of it? But I decided to go with it—what was the worst that could happen?

The witching hour approached. Before long we were back in the jungle lying on our backs with a gut full of ayahuasca, waiting for it to kick in. I couldn't hold the visions at bay for long; they came in waves, and I went under, drawn into the swirling vortex of texture, shape, and color.

One of my original intentions had been: How can I come back from the war and stay inspired? I had to push that question aside and focus on the intention Andreas had given. It was a struggle. As the visions rocketed I went through another gratitude list. Stay centered, I told myself. Everything seems perfect. Everything as it should be. I was reluctant to invoke the intention that Andreas had given, but I had to assume he had given it to me for a reason. So intoning inwardly, eyes still shut, I finally muttered, "Show me something that is not perfect."

Almost immediately, I caught sight of the silhouette of a figure moving like an apparition around the edge of the clearing. As it came nearer, I could see it more clearly—the blackest black I had ever seen. Beyond darkness—an obsidian portal into a black hole, as devoid of light as the farthest reaches of outer space. Almost hypnotized, I strained to make sure that what I was seeing was real, staring at the specter with wide-eyed alarm. It crept closer, and within the expanse of its blackness was an intricate geometry of quivering color—a circuit-board pattern of shimmering energy. The specter crept closer still. When it was almost on top of me, it paused and knelt on one knee beside the person lying to my left. The specter was Ben! I felt immense relief, but I also was shocked by his transformation into a kind of energy being. I heard him whisper into the person's ear next to me. Then he stood up. He was spectacular. But no—this *could not* be true! He had donned a hooded black mask and now wore a cloak made of the thinnest gossamer. The cloak had a wispy silver tinge, so very thin it draped over his head all the way to the ground like a man-sized cobweb. I could still make out his muscular build through this filigree cloak. *Holy fucking mother of God, he has actually changed into a superhero's outfit!* The mythic voyage had gone too far now. Andreas stepped over the line and into the ludicrous, taking the event way over the top, enacting a crazy pantomime, complete with costumes.

Ten minutes later Ben came over to me, and he was, of course, completely normal. The stage-show light costume was gone. He was dressed in his usual cargo shorts and a dark maroon vest. I had to have a quiet word with myself, embarrassed somehow without even speaking at the sheer overblown ridiculousness of the hallucination. *Right sunshine, you've been hallucinating very powerfully indeed. Get a grip!*

Half an hour later, still lying on the mattress, I was startled by the sound of footsteps directly behind me. Twigs snapped, leaves crunched—someone was standing inches from my scalp. A shape swooped, momentarily blocking out the trees and night sky. It was Ben again. He leaned down, placing one hand on my chest, over my heart, pressing firmly. Then he whispered so that no one else could hear. "Absolutely fantastic. So, so good."

Elation swept through me like a rush of warm water. This was completely outside my experience of manhood. Marines never did this to each other—overtly displaying sentiment like this—and I felt an entirely different level of brotherly love.

A little later I heard footfall behind me again, the crunching heavier this time. A huge mass blocked out the canopy. Adrenaline spiked as the looming shape squatted, and I felt the weight of two mighty hands pressing on my chest over my heart. It was Andreas. Without speaking, he put his mouth to my heart and sucked loudly, with all his might. The inhalation lasted several seconds before he lifted his head, exhaling noisily, spewing out air up to the canopy as if it contained a foul toxin. I was mystified but felt better for it. Then he crept away quietly without saying a word.

Soon Ben crept up again. He put one hand over my heart and whispered in my ear, "The child that is the *real* you inside will forever and ever keep you young. Forever and ever and ever and ever and ever . . ." Then he melted back into the darkness.

Belinda, one of the young twins, was lying on the mattress on the other side of me. She had cocooned herself in a sleeping bag to keep the mosquitoes off and feel secure. We were a couple of hours into the ceremony, and I hadn't noticed her move. No fidgeting or sighs, no purging—nothing, as silent as a pharaoh in a sarcophagus. Very odd. She must be cooking—it had to be 100°F in there.

As if reading my mind, she ripped open the sleeping bag and scrambled out. She was wearing several layers and a baggy jumper. She repositioned herself on top of her sleeping bag and began to make *ahhh* sounds. I'd grown used to them by now. Hearing the strange elocutions of what sounded like mystical ecstasy had taken some getting used to but by now were commonplace.

Belinda sighed softly, "Ahhhhhh." Then the sound became more frequent, increasing in volume and urgency, intense and insistent. "Ahhhhhhhhh!" Loud enough now to properly disturb the entire group, the sort of sound you'd make if you stubbed your toe or were being pinched.

"AHHHHHHHHHHHHH!"

Then she screamed, long and loud! It must have been 120 decibels, violently piercing the air and shattering the peace. She screamed over and over. I was shocked out of my wits, realizing instantly that I'd never before heard an adult woman scream right next to me. Ben hurried over, made a quick assessment, then squatted next to her. "Belinda, go inside! Be quiet! Go inside!"

But she wasn't listening and started sobbing. She got up on her knees reaching out, trying to hold him.

"No, Belinda!" he hissed. "Lie back down—now!"

Every fiber of my being was straining with the urge to leap up and help, to offer some kind of comfort, but I stayed put, as did everyone else. We followed Andreas's admonition to not help when someone was in distress—leave it to him and his crew.

Ben held Belinda's wrists and guided her back down to a prone position on the mattress. As soon as he touched her, she began to giggle hysterically.

"Lie down and focus on your intention. You *know* who you are. Go inside!" he urged.

The noises that emanated from her next were truly disturbing. Hysteria morphing between laughter, pain, and terror, circling back to unsettling laughter. I couldn't shake the feeling that while Belinda had been cocooned in her bag something had entered her—a disembodied entity, a bad one, and it was now wreaking havoc. I had no personal experience, but I'd seen enough films to get a hunch something demonic was among us. She was up again now on her feet, wailing in anguish, the pain she was suffering obviously a torture.

Was it true that in this environment, with this dose of ayahuasca, and with all of us being so open to all possibilities, our intentions could have an effect not just on us but on other people, too? Perhaps intentions weren't mere thoughts or *only* thoughts. They had their own form. What kind of sorcery was this? For the first time I believed I was witnessing something blatantly paranormal.

We now had a full-blown crisis on our hands, hurtling from bizarre to shocking. The Shipibo shamanas had stopped singing and moved as a group to huddle around Belinda, a few of them attempting to lay her back down. They were chattering loudly, their tone full of urgency and concern. Andreas and Alfredo appeared, followed by César, the head ayahuasquero—now a dozen or more people huddled around her.

With a cold horror I realized that there was a pattern emerging. Every time I had been next to a woman during an ayahuasca ceremony, the woman either became catatonic (as Miley had at La Kapok Center) or appeared to become possessed. Was I the unwitting host to bad energy brought back from Helmand?

Belinda's groans sounded utterly inhuman. I was sure that something malevolent was among us. Ben tried to get her to drink some water, but she snatched the bottle, sucked the fluid, and then spat it over his face, laughing hysterically. Poor girl. I pleaded inwardly, gravely worried, *Please come back. Please.*

César blew sacred tobacco smoke over her head, chest, and back in an attempt to cleanse her. The Shipibo women began to sing soothingly. Her hysterical laughter began to shift into long drawn-out wailing then degenerated into wracking sobs. The hysteria continued for another ten minutes before the combined work had an effect. César's shamanic ministrations, the Shipibo women's icaros, and Ben's presence finally helped her regain composure. Or maybe by now she was just exhausted. She collapsed back down to her knees, her cries constrained until they once again became the *ahhh* sound. After a while she quieted down until she was merely whimpering.

Occasionally she laughed. There seemed to be some sort of telepathic connection between her and her twin, Ruth. They were lying twenty meters apart, but when Ruth giggled—obviously off in her own world—inexplicably Belinda's arm would raise up high into the air like something was pulling it—or rather yanking it violently—like a puppet, and it remained there for the duration of Ruth's giggle and not a moment longer. As soon as Ruth's giggling stopped, Belinda's arm flopped down heavily. The connection also worked in reverse. When Belinda giggled, in less than a single second we'd hear Ruth giggle too. Spooky.

Belinda finally became calm. It had taken a momentous effort for me to stay still and remain lying down while all the commotion had gone on within five feet. I felt relieved when the ceremony ended thirty minutes later. At the end of each ceremony, Andreas and Ben sang the same lullaby, and the more experienced voyagers would join in. The first lines of it were: "Like ripples on the ocean, they go around forever . . . Forever and ever, like a circle in the water." Ben then played a tune of orchestral quality on his flute.

I was glad it was over. This ceremony's second half had been horrendous. I looked over to Belinda and could hardly believe that she was fully conscious, now standing packing her kit away, like nothing had happened.

"You OK?" I asked.

"Yeah, sure," she said. She even smiled.

I wanted to shout "Do you *realize* what just fucking *happened*? You were in the midst of a full-blown possession back there!" I didn't push it—more distress was the last thing any of us needed. But I was troubled. At the opening of the ceremony, my mind had asked, "Show me something that isn't perfect," and I had concentrated on that for half an hour. Look what happened—something hellish! Her episode was as opposite of perfect as anything I could think of. Had I somehow been at least partially responsible for manifesting this crisis? What had Andreas been thinking to give such an intention? Had he *known* this would result? What *was* he exactly? Twenty-first-century wizard? White witch doctor? Psycho or savior? Mental or mentor? I was wracked by doubt. What were we *really* doing here? What the hell was going on? Trust, which I had just recently recovered, was again on shaky ground. This wasn't a cult, but I had to admit that it was cultish. Intense visions, intentions that appeared to come true, and entities that took possession—there was no doubt that events on this journey had exceeded the limits of rationality. Things could evolve from "songs of praise" to "fright night" in one stormy psychedelic channel change. Everything about ayahuasca, Andreas, and the argonauts suddenly seemed inexplicable. I realized that Helmand wasn't the only place I'd been to recently that had a heart of darkness.

I flipped my torch up to Belinda's face. A beautiful girl—but one who now looked as though she had been battered by a hurricane. Sweat covered her skin, long brown hair plastered her face. Yet her eyes were lucid and clear, and she seemed OK, despite the dishevelment.

On the way back to the canoe, I figured now was as good a time as any to get a closer look at an unusual kapok tree that had caught the group's attention when we had come into the clearing. It was gigantic, a fortress of integrity, ramrod straight with an immense circumference. Ten people linked hand by hand would be unable to encircle it. Smooth root webs rose ten feet aboveground, forming cavernous spaces capable of sheltering several people. I stepped between two of the largest roots, put both hands on the trunk, and gazed up. The trunk rose magnificently before the canopy fanned out, seemingly a hundred meters up.

Then it just kept going, higher and higher. I had never seen a living thing project such majesty.

I noticed something fascinating. Six inches above my forehead an intricate symmetrical pattern, nearly a foot wide, had been carved into the bark. It also looked relatively fresh, chiseled within the last year or two. The design was reminiscent of classic ayahuasca-inspired visions, the same style seen on the artwork of the indigenous people. The hairs on the back of my neck rose. We had stumbled upon a tree that had been marked by indigenous people passing through, perhaps on a hunting trip and now long gone. It had been obvious that those unknowns had taken the utmost care crafting their carvings. Whoever had marked this giant must have felt the reverence and awe it was also inspiring in me. I decided that it was just the thing to help ground Belinda. I walked over to where she was standing, Ben alongside her.

"Come over and have a look at this," I beckoned. "You won't believe your eyes."

I held Belinda's elbow and gently guided her, while Ben followed behind us. She was extremely unsteady and wobbled and giggled as I led her. "OK," I directed, "face the trunk. Put your hands on it at shoulder height, really feel it—and then slowly, slowly look up."

"Wow! Oh, my God! Wow!"

Seconds later I drew her attention from the canopy down the trunk to the carved symbol just above her forehead. "Now, look at this . . ."

She stared blankly for a moment, the significance sinking in. Then her eyes widened, as wide and circular as an archery target. She nodded slightly, almost imperceptibly. Our faces were only a couple of feet apart, our eyes locked for a few moments. I wanted her to know, without telling her, that I understood that she'd just gone through something momentous, and now she was safe, back here on Mother Earth, among nature and friends.

Ben broke the spell, stepping forward to look. "Wow! Oh, my God!" His face broke into a huge smile, "Dude, that is awesome!"

We finally pulled ourselves away from the tree and headed back with the others to the canoe, and before long we were back on the ship, another day of the Mythic Voyage complete.

Months later, back home, during a phone call to catch up on news, I was able to hear Belinda's version of her possession. Up until this phone call, it appeared that she had been taken over by an entity, and this was what had caused all her anguish and hence her screams. But according to her, nothing like that had happened. It had been nothing nefarious or supernatural. What she actually experienced was access to the trauma of childhood memories, when she had felt abandoned by her parents, scared, and helpless. She also had regressed to a time in her childhood before she could even talk, and during the reliving of it, under the influence of ayahuasca, she felt overtaken by darkness—a bad memory, not an entity—that she had no control over. It was a direct communication with her subconscious. She had screamed because she was drawn through a doorway back into this pain, and there was no way to get back. She said she was deeply thankful for Ben's intervention. Through him she had found her way through the darkness, back to the present. When Ben had insistently reminded her, "Belinda, you know who you are!" she regained her power. But until that moment she had never felt so overwhelmed and powerless.

She related details of her childhood—her parents' battle with alcoholism and her father's abandonment when the twins were eight. Although she had her twin sister for support, she felt unseen as a child, unheard, and invisible. She had repressed much of that anguish, and she felt that the repressed emotion had displayed itself in her body, the tension causing her to have a constantly painful shoulder. So it was a possession of a kind—the possession of disempowering, painful memories. Her intention on the night of the ceremony had been to "feel trust in men again." She believed ayahuasca provided her the perfect journey into the self to do that, enabling her to trust in the masculine again, to release her fear of abandonment. Ben's presence had helped with this.

Despite the fact that she had been hysterical, she had felt the support of everybody in the circle. She told me she felt I had provided an aura of safety. No one had ever said that to me before. She described how good it felt to scream that night—to let out all the repressed anger and fear. She said that she had actually been proactive, "calling it in" to happen. It was interesting to hear that since that night she had had no further pain or problem with her shoulder. She was grateful for the experience and felt that through this healing she was now "ten times stronger." She said ayahuasca helped heal her.

20

What Is God?

The next day, the final day of the voyage, I saw Andreas for a consultation. I wanted to speak to him about David R. Hawkins's power versus force theory, eager to hear his views on how a person might become enlightened.

I had read an unforgettable book called *Power versus Force* by Hawkins, and it played on my mind. To simplify greatly, Hawkins said that most people throughout history have operated through self-preservation, seeking safety and fulfillment at the expense of others. They tend to operate through control and domination, violence, manipulation, and coercion. But as people evolve in consciousness, they move up in awareness, operating from reason, joy, and empathy—the more positive emotions. They move from relying on force to being able to judiciously experience power. Power in this context meant tolerance, cooperation, understanding, and love. *Power* is the awesome state of nature, where the inferior efforts of humanity were equivalent to *force*.

Based on my experience with psychedelics, rather than from anything I learned from religion, I had begun to sense this natural universal power much more profoundly. Life had granted me the experience of both force (the military) and natural power (the Amazon and ayahuasca). Force typically achieved short-term gains but generally did not last over the long term. Work with entheogens was showing another way—power through expansion of consciousness. This path revealed power in its spiritual sense: a natural intelligence/consciousness, supremely greater than humanity, benevolent and awe-inspiring, the animating energy of the universe, the web of life of which we all are a part and from which we can never be disconnected.

Hawkins had a successful psychiatry practice in New York for over thirty years. His theory was that all human beings can be measured using a technique called applied kinesiology to gauge where they sit on a linear scale of consciousness, ranging from 1 to 1,000, similar to the electromagnetic spectrum. Thus, a person's consciousness can be measured on a scale (these numbers are an abbreviated summary): shame (20), apathy (50), fear (100), anger (150), courage (200), reason (400), unconditional love (500), peace (600), enlightenment (700–1,000). Mystics and holy men like Krishna, Mohammed, Jesus, and Buddha were extremely rare and were on the scale at over 700. Most of humanity scored at around the 200 mark. It seemed an outlandish theory but was interesting. His book had sold millions of copies and captured imaginations worldwide.

Hawkins wrote about an experience he had at age twelve when, through a near-death experience, he was in a state of being that he describes as "a suffusion of love that was beyond all description, beyond exquisite—that was timeless. . . . I knew that this was my reality. It melted my personal self into a form of non-existence into the infinite power of the love, which was overwhelming. It was a state of bliss."

I was curious if Andreas agreed with Hawkins's scale of consciousness, applying as it did not just to individuals but the entire human race. Based on the scale I wondered if there were groups of people, or even entire populations, that lagged behind others precisely because they were attached to a group. I explained the concept to him, then asked his opinion. He looked troubled, and after a long pause sighed, saying, "Yes, I've heard of this book and this scale of spiritual measurement. Within our culture we are obsessed with measurement. But it is very wrong to measure spirituality in this ridiculously linear and simplistic way. In fact, I'd say that this is monstrous!"

Melodramatic. Evidently, I'd overestimated my ability to articulate the essence of the book.

"What do you mean?"

"Imagine this situation." He positioned some objects—cups, a water glass, knives, forks, a pair of glasses—on the table between us, then explained, embellishing his discourse with the objects closest to hand.

"Let's say we have the Light over here," he said, placing the water glass at a point far up the table. The Light obviously meant a supreme universal intelligence. He then pointed to the various everyday objects on the table and gave a symbolic meaning to each as he moved them around. "Then you can have a pope over here, a teacher over here, a young boy over here, and an alcoholic tramp over here. Now, if I move each one steadily, incrementally, toward the Light that sits over here in this direction, and then I *stop* moving them—when I finish, which one is *now* closest to the light?"

A trick question, but hey, let's play the game.

"Well, it's this one," I said, picking up the cup that represented the boy, "because you've moved him closest to the Light." I moved the cup so that it was adjacent to the water glass, almost touching it.

"No!" he said. "He is *not* nearest the light. They are all the same. No man is nearer to God than another. God is all pervasive, omnipotent. God is everywhere, in all of us all of the time. God *is* existence."

This was the first time I had heard him ever explicitly mention the *G* word.

"So to use the scale in the book you speak about," he went on, "to say that you start out in life on a path and you must strive to progress along that path in incremental steps toward enlightenment is wrong—very wrong. The Light is in all of us all of the time. An innate power residing in everyone, a higher force, intangible, immeasurable, fundamentally composed of love. God lives within us and we within it."

I still thought Hawkins was on to something, especially after what

I witnessed in Afghanistan. The tribal beliefs in pride, revenge, and shame were core pillars of their value system. The extremes to which they took these beliefs exceeded anything I had experienced before. It is a country, like others in that part of the world, where Pashtunwali is the tribal code of life. The code originated with the Pashtun peoples in pre-Islamic times and continues to this day, stretching far and wide in the tribal areas of countries across the region. Part of that code is *badal* (justice). If someone is killed, the family must avenge that murder by killing the perpetrator. Doing so is a matter of honor—and honor, in their eyes, is sacrosanct. But then the family of the man killed in revenge has an obligation to the same code, so they must defend their honor and avenge his killing. It was a generational vicious circle of feuds and violence. To me this code is rooted in scarcity, shame, and anger. After time spent in rural Afghanistan, I had come to believe that such codes persisted because of the endemic poverty. Fear stunts growth and cultural development; it breeds conflict and separation—an us-versus-them mentality. The result is that people operate from force (coercion, domination) rather than power (empathy, cooperation). Since I had come to the Amazon and begun working with ayahuasca, I was beginning to comprehend what natural power could really mean. In a short space of time, I had traveled the spectrum from force to power, having left the desolation of desert, stepping now into the abundance of the jungle.

I knew I didn't have much time, as others were waiting for their consultations. I was considering what to ask next when Andreas did something unexpected. He told me about himself. Following a painful and troubled childhood, fraught with conflict and social exclusion, his salvation was delivered at age thirteen with a letter from his school announcing that he had been tested and was to be accepted into Mensa. They placed him squarely in the "potential genius" zone and the redemption was that, at last, he was perceived by all—family, teachers, peers—as a gifted child with an extraordinarily high IQ. Andreas then went on to tell me how, as an adult, following significant success, a series of events combined to bring everything crashing down. Life as he knew it was lost, and it was an internal shift that saved him.

"I was a successful entrepreneur, with five different businesses. One was a clothing factory that provided a national sports team with their uniforms. But my health had deteriorated terribly. I suffered more than forty minor strokes and had a chronic problem with my blood that made it coagulate unnecessarily. That problem had its own side effect—causing me to put on weight. At times I ballooned to more than 350 pounds. I starved myself to get my weight down, eating solid food only on Saturdays. Even then I'd still put on five pounds a week. Due to these illnesses my businesses began to suffer. To make matters worse my wife left me, deciding she could no longer cope. I later found out she was having an affair. In any event, she left me, taking our two sons with her. At the same time I had an accident while walking in the street in which someone smashed into my knee, breaking it. I was wheelchair-bound for six months. After an operation on my knee, I became house-bound while recovering and so couldn't work. My businesses further deteriorated. I developed a fever and a urinary infection, which made pissing feel like passing molten lead. Every five minutes or so, one or two drops of black liquid would ooze out the end of my dick, which was intensely painful. I was unable to take any painkillers because they interfered with my stroke medicine. Then my body temperature began to fluctuate wildly, from fever to chills, swinging from 107.6 to 89.6°F. I felt I was losing my mind. Then I discovered that taking aspirin helped with the fever and so afforded me a two-hour period of lucidity. During one of these periods of clarity, I had an epiphany. I realized that I could change something—my mind! I could be happy simply by choosing to be. Of course, almost as soon as I had that insight, I doubted it. I asked myself, 'Can I be really happy like this? With the urinary infection, smashed knee, blood/weight disorder, multiple strokes, fever, my family lost, and businesses in ruins?' I decided I could—I could be happy. I began to laugh at myself, because I knew from that moment on, despite all outward appearances of pain and chaos, I was going to be happy.

I underwent a transformational shift in consciousness, and from that moment on—and I can genuinely pin it down to that single moment—my way of being in the world shifted. I began rebuilding my life based on this newfound happiness."

He took a breath from the lengthy monologue. He had served up his personal information and now wanted payback.

"Tell me, Alex, why did you come on the Mythic Voyage?"

"To see the Amazon."

"Come *on,* let's get real! I think we both know that there are reasons that a man does something and then there are the *real* reasons. What was your real intention?"

I fumbled for a moment. "Er . . . to be happy?" Why had I phrased my answer as a question?

"To be happy," he echoed, arching an eyebrow. He sat in silence for a while looking troubled and extremely unhappy with that answer. "Really? OK, but let's take a step back, shall we? Tell me again, why did you go to Afghanistan?"

I rattled off my reasons. "Adventure. To do some good in the world, to set an example for my kids. To help people—since we've been there, more than two million girls have been able to go to school."

He looked intensely irritated, waving the comments away with a derisive sweep of his arm. "Yeah, yeah. I heard it all before from you. Don't give me the same shit. I don't give a fuck about the suffering of the Afghan people right now. This is bullshit! These are bullshit reasons!" He paused ever so briefly before continuing. "What about your wife? What the hell did she think about you choosing to abandon her and the children? What were you thinking?"

Now put on the defensive, my first thought was that other married men with children went to war and always had. I said, "Andreas, it was all fine! Honestly. I took care of business—arranging everything before I left. I made sure that if I was killed there'd be enough insurance to pay for the house and leave some extra cash. If I was killed, I felt pretty sure my wife would find somebody else to love and to take care of the children. And, besides, as a man I felt I really needed to do this."

He stared back in revulsion. Then he spoke slowly, very deliberately, enunciating every word, each syllable—it felt like a bitch slap and his words stung. "So you devalued yourself so much that you reduced yourself to an *insurance* payment?" He shook his head in disbelief. "That is so fucked up! You assumed that your wife and children wouldn't miss you? That if you were killed, you wouldn't leave a hole in their lives? Do you really think so *little* of yourself that you mean practically nothing to them? Do you really believe this?"

His face was now a mask of shock and contempt. I had never seen anyone look at me that way, and I felt the flush of confusion and shame rising up as heat to my face. I had sounded clinical, unfeeling—that's not what I'd meant. The impact of his words left me speechless.

He sat back on his chair, his palms on his thighs, his head tilted upward so that his eyes locked onto mine. Out of the blue he said, "OK, so tonight . . . I have been thinking . . . I want *you* to run the ceremony!"

My mind reeled. *Run* the ceremony? What the hell was he saying? He continued as if reading my mind, a common occurrence lately. "Alex, there is a hole inside of you. I can feel it. You need to fill it. So I feel it will benefit you greatly if tonight you run the ceremony. I have never asked another person to do this on any Mythic Voyage before, but it is what you need. I trust my instincts. You will be fine. You don't have to if you don't want to. The choice is yours."

I didn't know what to say. He pushed on, explaining that the key difference for me would be that by leading the ceremony I would have to help with everybody else's needs. If they needed water, help to the toilet, had a breakdown, or needed comforting words—it would be my responsibility to give it. He said it would be virtuous, and I would have to try to appreciate that when I helped others, I was also helping myself.

"This is good!" he exclaimed. "It is self-serving."

He went on to suggest that my intention for the ceremony should be: *Show me what it feels like to have intense pleasure.* He explained,

"Knowing and experiencing intense pleasure will provide you with a taste of what it feels like to become enlightened."

Feeling both privileged and daunted, I thought about his offer for a few minutes. "OK. I'll do it . . . although what if I need some help?"

"Don't worry, I'll be there, and Ben, too. We will both be there for you."

I said OK again, although I immediately started questioning the wisdom of doing this. What if I made a mistake? I had no training. There was absolutely no doubt I'd be having powerful hallucinations of my own. I had participated in ceremonies but didn't know how to run one. Tonight's was in only four hours—barely time to get used to the idea, never mind prepare. I thought about reneging—and then just as quickly thought, "You will never have this opportunity again." Andreas indicated the matter was settled by ending our meeting. He repeated the intention I should hold, "Show me what it feels like to have intense pleasure."

As I rose to leave, he tapped his finger on his chest, where his big fat heart beat beneath his big fat frame. As I opened the door to leave the room, he said, "And remember, Alex. The best gift you can give to your children is to show them a happy father."

21

The Most Amazing Night

As I waited to board the canoe to go ashore for the final ceremony, Stergiani approached, her brow furrowed. Without any context she asked, "How do you cope?"

"What do you mean?"

"What do you do to get through each ceremony?"

I thought about it. "You know what? I do this . . ." I put my hands together in prayer formation, the tips of my fingers pressed lightly against each other, but palms slightly apart. Like an upside-down heart, or a mushroom, or a pyramid—take your pick. "I don't know why, but I find it helps. And sometimes I lay my hand across my heart while thinking about my intention. And when things get too intense, I force myself to smile. Force it. The sensation over my face has a psychological effect, makes me feel better, slightly stronger, able to cope."

When we were finally seated in the canoe, she leaned in silently, resting the side of her head on my upper arm. She stayed close, but neither of us said another word during the ride. We were both nervous.

Ben had chosen a good spot. We gathered in the clearing, and I took a long look around. From now on I was supposed to be running the show. Everything was in place: the mattresses and puke buckets were arranged in a circle along the edge of the clearing, and a toilet area had been hacked out of the bush. César and the shamanas were gathered in a group. The jug of ayahuasca and a clutter of cups sat on a blanket in front of César. Just looking at the jug made the corners of my mouth turn down in disgust, and my body practically shuddered at the very thought of once again swallowing the bitter brew.

Once we had all drunk a cup, everyone settled into their places. The shamanas began to sing an icaro. I stood off to one side feeling awkward and unsure, not knowing what to expect or do exactly. Andreas made an announcement to everyone that I would be leading the ceremony and then, thankfully, came over and gave me some instructions. If anybody cried out for help and called for him, I was to go to that person and say, "Tonight *I'm* Andreas. I'm here to help. What do you need?"

He escorted me to his chair, which was positioned just beyond the perimeter of the circle so that anyone sitting in it had a commanding view of the space. "Sit in this chair and watch over," he said.

I took his seat, appreciating the line of sight into the ceremony. I'd never seen the space from the outside, and it was daunting to see twenty people laid out flat on their backs. The eight Shipibo women sat in a line, singing. César was at one end of the line, his deeper timbre entwining perfectly with the higher pitch of the shamanas.

Waves of nausea pulsed through me, partly ayahuasca, partly nerves. Visions came on fast and hard. My mind was in upheaval, and soon my stomach followed suit, the nausea rising again. I grabbed a bucket, but just as quickly put it back down empty. I didn't want to disturb the people lying just in front of my chair, so I trotted into the brush and puked there. Midretch, I heard Andreas. "Alex, please come here."

I wiped my mouth roughly on the back of my sleeve, took a swig of water, and staggered over. The jungle spun wildly, and I could hardly walk in a straight line. His voice was superhumanly deep, an earthquake in human form, and he gripped my shoulders tightly, his face only a few inches from mine. "Listen to me carefully. Pay close attention!" Sounding deadly serious, he shook my shoulders as reinforcement. "I want you to go to each person and offer them words of comfort throughout the night. If anybody cries out, remember tonight *you* are me. And make sure you walk quietly around the perimeter when you approach them. If you need to be sick, then be sick. But make sure you fulfill your duty! Can you do this? Can you conduct yourself in a way that is mythic?"

His huge black outline stood before me. The forest surrounding us continued to spin wildly. Inexplicable shapes—part carnivalesque, part animated fauna—swarmed everywhere. Colored lights popped in and out of existence. I fought the urge to be sick again—it was too much. Sensing a dent in my resolve, he shook me again, and rumbled, "My brother, can you do this?'

I was a grown man, yet he made me feel like a callow adolescent. "Yes."

"Good. Now listen! Ben will not be able to help you tonight. He has a special task of his own to fulfill. He has his own demon he needs to deal with, and that is what he will do. He has now gone inside himself. You cannot count on him to help you."

I groaned. Bollocks! I'd been counting on Ben tonight. Now, spinning out, with the prospect of support withering, I pleaded inwardly that this night wouldn't erupt into a dark ordeal. My mind then raced back to something Richard, at La Kapok Center, had said "People are entrusting their souls to us." I glanced over to where Ben was lying on a mattress in the circle. I could barely make out his form, his arms folded across his chest. Jesus, this was going to be monumental. I fought the urge to puke my guts out, and with mind spinning I wondered how Andreas and Ben coped, dispensing compassion and kindness throughout the ceremony while tripping on a gut full of ayahuasca. My admiration rose to new heights.

I bumbled back to the chair. Everywhere I looked kaleidoscopic colors sparked out of the darkness, intricate patterns drenched everything, the air was saturated with pulsing energy as if it were alive. Synesthesia enveloped me; colors and shapes had sounds; senses crossed wildly. I began to seriously doubt that I could cope. I sat down in the chair and breathed deeply; trying to control it all helped me to settle my bewilderment. Taking stock, I regained my bearings. This was supposed to be a privilege . . .

It wasn't long before I heard the first person cry out. "Andreas!'

I sprang to my feet. It was Julian, the American. I made my way over as quietly as I could.

"Julian, it's Alex. Listen! Tonight I'm running the ceremony, remember? If you need Andreas, I'm acting on his behalf. I can give you whatever you need. How can I help?"

"It's my chest. It feels tight."

I ran my torchlight along the length of his body. He was wrapped up unnecessarily tightly in too many layers and covered with a blanket. "OK, you're overheating. Believe me, I know what that's like. Take off the blanket, remove your coat—there's no need to boil up. Just keep your T-shirt on and keep the blanket draped over your top half. It'll keep the insects off."

Once he was comfortable, I walked into the middle of the circle and took a long moment to reflect. I was surrounded by twenty souls journeying under the influence of one of the most powerful psychedelics on the planet, each sending out their own strong personal intentions for insight, healing, and hope. My own mind was reeling from the ayahuasca. Despite the eye-popping alchemy, I was sober enough to appreciate that I was able to move about at will—still able to think and talk. I felt responsible for the welfare of the people around me. We were in the world's largest rainforest, camped next to the most powerful river on Earth. The moon beamed expansively, its power reaching down—it had to be seen to be believed, like a smaller version of the sun. The shamanas were singing beautifully, their songs sounding as natural as the insects and frogs of the jungle. It was perfect. I embraced it, and my arms instinctively reached up to the sky, stretching toward the moon. I could *feel* the energy from the atmosphere seeping into me as a potent power. The straighter my arms stretched skyward, the more energy I felt channeled down and into me. It was enchanting. I dropped my arms and walked over to the shamanas and faced them. My hands moved together into a prayer position, and I bowed the lowest bow of my life, a bow infused with respect and endless gratitude. Words cannot express the love and sincerity I felt. I bowed over and over. The power of their icaros was incredible: I stood in front of a wall of fluid sound energy that reverberated through me. In contrast, the prospect of assuaging an angry god with pathetic human negotiation was revealed as ridiculous historical folly. Surrender. Yield. Accept this is the path for infinite power—the supreme benevolence.

With growing delight I realized that what I was feeling was *intense pleasure*. The intention was working! I was on a rocket ship of pleasure, propelled on a course to the heart of the ineffable. Artists and musicians have navigated these realms for millennia, and I had become an initiate.

The insight led me to turn to bow to all of the voyagers, one by one. There was that feeling again—a compelling feeling of interconnectedness. This wasn't about me. It was about *us*. We are evolving into a single global civilization. The Internet is proving this. A collaborative, always on, planetary hive mind.

I checked on everyone individually, walking as stealthily as I could around the outside of the circle, wearing battered old desert combat trousers. I felt like the ex-marine in the film *Avatar* (the opening line of the movie is "There's no such thing as an ex-marine") when he lands for the first time in a rainforest on a new world, in his avatar body. He had physically regenerated, and in his new environment everything looked different. I too, felt as if I were in an avatar body. I looked the same but inwardly had changed. And like the rainforest in the movie, while I was under the influence of ayahuasca, the Amazon around me was captivatingly bizarre and beautiful.

I knelt beside Robert and put my hand on his heart, bent my head close to his ear, and said, "Trust. Truth. Peace. Forever and ever and ever and ever . . ."

I put my hand on Giselle's heart whispering, "You are perfect and always will be. Love lives inside of you. You are love."

Clearly, when it comes to compassionate creativity, I was no heavy-weight, but I was doing my best under the circumstances, with all my senses reeling and my heart wide open. At times I felt completely connected, at others conspicuously inept. I'm no holy man, no shaman. Those skills take years of hard training to acquire, and I'd had no such training. When self-doubt or feelings of inadequacy crept back, I forced myself to be mindful that I was imposing limiting beliefs on myself, and I recovered the capacity to be compassionate.

I saw someone sit up on the far side of the circle. It was Pietro. I walked over putting my arm around his shoulder. "Pietro, are you OK? Do you need anything?'

"My bucket . . ."

I passed him the bucket, and he puked hard into it, the harshness competing with the ethereal sound of the icaro. Robert was sitting up, too, and I heard him purge. It was often like that—one person's retching would set off a daisy chain of vomiting.

Everything was going smoothly until I noticed the silhouette of someone else sitting up. I went over to investigate and found Anna, obviously in distress. She had her head in her hands. Peering through the dark, we looked at each other. Her eyes pleaded with mine as she uttered words I will never forget. She stared up from her mattress at me and implored, "Suck it out!"

"I'm sorry—what?"

No chance that I'd misheard. She begged. "Please, please, just suck it out!"

Jesus Christ—my eyes rolled under the cover of darkness—*you have got to be fucking kidding! I am in* way *over my head here!* I didn't have the knowledge to suck out a bad spirit, or whatever it was, from a troubled woman in the throes of powerful visions.

"You need to stare it down, Anna. Face it! This is not an option. Don't let it feed on your fear. Give it your full attention! Don't let it deceive you. Tell yourself everything is as it should be."

But she was getting more desperate by the moment. I had to do something. So I composed myself, grasped her head with both hands over her ears, bent my head, and burrowed my face deep into the hair on the top of her head—and sucked. I sucked and sucked as hard as I could—deep, deep, deep. Then exhaled with equal power, spewing out every remnant of anything energetic that I'd inhaled that could be spiritually foul. I wasn't taking any risks, making sure every vestige of air sucked in was spat out. I repeated the process several more times. After several attempts, it was clear that I'd failed. She was still writhing and in considerable distress. I sucked at sucking. Time to get help.

I found Andreas and explained. He listened intently, his response typically oblique. "You must stand tall like a God and have confidence to face any man—or anything—anywhere. I know you have this capability. Do you understand me? Do you *believe* me? Tonight you must *become* mythic!"

I understood, but believing him was an entirely different matter. No doubt he'd be great for morale in a firefight, but right here, right now, spirits appeared to be swarming, not bullets.

Luckily his appraisal of the situation included more than just little ole me fronting it out against her demon. He directed me to go to César and get his help. I suspected that César was about to perform the Shipibo shamanic equivalent of an exorcism. Relief surged—everything was going to be OK. We had a plan. I could do this with César's help. I really didn't know Anna that well and wasn't entirely convinced that it was a bad spirit causing her distress. In all likelihood, Anna was manifesting some psychological issue that ayahuasca was exacerbating. But the shaman in me wouldn't be fully squelched. If this *was* a possession, I wanted help.

I went to César to explain, and he set about preparing a pungent plant potion with various leaves that he had at hand. When he was done he called three of the Shipibo women over, and the five of us went over to Anna, who was still sitting with her hands over her face, her body rocking back and forth. As we stood in a circle around her, she pleaded, "Get it out! Please get it out!"

The shamanas muttered among themselves for a moment and then sang. While they sang one of them stopped and flicked liquids over Anna or blew tobacco over her. This went on for about five minutes. I left them to it and went to Andreas to let him know how things were going. He wasn't perturbed in the slightest, sitting like an emperor on a throne, composed and unruffled. As far as he was concerned, exorcisms in the jungle were to be expected. When a possession occurred it was merely something to be dealt with.

By this time I was certain that everyone must be feeling the same—spinning out in psychedelia, a phantasia of colors, an irrefutable sense that magic was happening.

Abruptly, Andreas grabbed my shoulders, his voice cracking with emotion. "Alex, I want you to go and get Josh and bring him to me. It is time for him to receive his blessing."

A blessing? What kind of blessing? Isn't that what priests do? The nearest priest had to be at least five hundred miles away! I stumbled over, coordination in bits, gently shaking his shoulder. "Josh, Andreas wants you to receive a blessing."

He sat bolt upright, then stood up unsteadily, and I escorted him over to where Andreas was sitting.

With all the melodrama of a king relinquishing his throne to a first-born son, Andreas said with the utmost solemnity, "Josh, you have been chosen tonight to receive a blessing from the shamanas. Are you ready?"

"Yes, Andreas."

Guiding Josh by the elbows, Andreas and I walked him over to where the remaining Shibipo women—the ones who weren't ministering to Anna—were sitting in a line, singing. We got within five feet of them when Andreas commanded, "Josh, kneel."

He knelt, as if for a knighthood. Andreas pushed him lower, head down so that his forehead was touching a mat on the ground. Josh stretched out his arms in front of him, placing his palms flat on the ground, adopting the ancient position of complete surrender. The women sang louder, with more intensity.

I left Josh with them and went back over to check on Anna. César and the three shamanas appeared to have been successful, as she was calmer. But when she looked up at me, her eyes still seemed to be pleading for help.

"Lie back down." I said. "You'll feel better if you just lie down and go inside."

"I can't—I just can't do it. Please."

"You must," I insisted. "It's so easy. All you have to do is focus on your intention. Just lie down."

Instead, she grabbed my leg, wrapping both arms around it, as if bracing against the only a tree in a hurricane. Another first. I had to peel her off my leg.

"I need the bathroom," she said.

Good. *This* I could deal with. "OK, I'll help you up. I'll walk with you."

She could hardly stand. I had to put one of her arms around my shoulders and support her weight. I led her to the cleared space in the brush, made sure she had a torch and toilet paper, and left her to it. Things were getting hectic back in the circle. I could hear people calling out for Andreas, crying out for assistance. Andreas called my name, and I trotted over like a faithful dog. "Please get Belinda and Eddie. I want them to receive their blessing."

I fetched them, and they underwent their blessing. My attention now split in multiple directions. People were calling for assistance, Andreas was asking me to collect people, and where the hell was Anna? It had been at least five minutes, and she hadn't returned. I went to check, and with a quick flick of the torch, I saw that she'd collapsed, trousers still around her knees. Jesus Christ not again. She could have fallen on a snake or an unforgiving trail of bullet ants. Collapsing unconsciously in the jungle—to be avoided at all costs. The "intense pleasure" had become a distant memory: now I was firefighting, triaging, deciding who to prioritize. I helped Anna back up, but it was a struggle, as she seemed barely conscious. I managed to get her back to her mattress, but still she wouldn't lie down. She clung to me, and I offered all the words of assurance that I could humanly muster. Then, with total incongruity, she let go, reached into her backpack, pulled out a cigarette, and lit it. At last she appeared to be fully present and calm as she smoked. Andreas's voice boomed across the clearing. "Alex!"

I found him. He reached out, gripping me tightly. "Would you like to receive a blessing?" He was extremely moved, his huge frame trembling with emotion. His voice cracked as he spoke, and tears were rolling down his cheeks.

"Yes," I replied, and we headed over to the shamanas.

I was in way over my head and speculating about everything. The three argonauts who'd already received a blessing were huddled together in a heap in the center of the circle. I could hear words emanating from their mass of entangled limbs, "Oh, my God! Wow! Whoa!" They were stroking and hugging each other, giddy with inebriation. This was turning out to be the maddest damned night! There were people here who think this is normal. Who in the "civilized" world would believe it?

Moments later I was on my knees. Andreas placed a hand on the back of my neck and pushed my head down until my forehead met the ground. As my head went down to meet the deck, I snatched a glimpse of the shamanas five feet in front. They were smiling, one or two were even giggling. A liquid was dripped over me, smelling of orange blossom, and it spilled down the side of my face, running off the end of my nose. The shamanas sang over me, their songs a benediction. I felt part of something ancient and sacred, a rare privilege to be savored. Two thoughts competed for my attention—*this is crazy, this is holy, this is crazy, this is holy.* Finally, César helped me to my feet and led me to the center of the circle to join the other three who'd already received blessings. Their writhing, the dark, and my inability to focus all combined to make the scene appear like a bizarre kind of clothed orgy. *Let it slide,* I told myself. *It isn't every day you get to experience a blessing while hallucinating in a jungle.* Even so, I was happy that this was the final night of the voyage. I couldn't take any more.

After the ceremony ended, as we chugged back in the canoe back to the ship, I heard a female voice in the dark but couldn't identify who spoke. "Congratulations Alex, you are now a warrior of light!'

I stayed silent, feeling unworthy. I didn't know what she meant exactly—and still don't. I settled back in the seat, gazing in rapt fascination at the looming mothership, now lit up with fairy lights, my fingertips trailing in the warm river water.

I was euphoric.

22

The Power of Choice

Religion is belief in someone else's experience, spirituality is having your own experience.

DEEPAK CHOPRA

My marine days are over. My Amazonian adventure complete—for now.

The military, like religions, has dogmatic rules and codes. Transgressions are harshly dealt with. By retelling this story it may only be a matter of time before I incur the military equivalent of Catholic excommunication. Altered states of consciousness are anathema to the armed forces. But what I learned in the Amazon was worth it. When disruptive ideas germinate they can surmount military force, and as history has shown sometimes they can do that without anyone getting hurt.

Before I left the Amazon, I had one more consultation with Andreas, back in the ship's library. During it, I felt ready to open up about my past. "Andreas, I think my decision to serve in the war and leave my family behind was linked to my ideas about masculinity and what it means to be a man. And I think the trouble I encountered as a child growing up with three fathers has something to do with that."

I paused to collect my thoughts.

"You see, I really don't know what it's like to feel love for a father. My mother got divorced three times. I had a violent stepfather through most of my childhood, and as far as I can remember, I never had a father tell me that he cared for me. I think my aggression and lack of value for my own life, which you mentioned yesterday, may have something to do with that."

When I paused all he said was, "Go on."

"My stepfather sold insurance for a living his whole adult life, and he really didn't have a clue about jack shit. I showed him a newspaper advert for the marines when I was twelve and asked for his opinion. He thought it was a joke and told me that they were a bunch of criminals, that I'd be stupid for even considering it. Years later I realized that I think he was probably confusing them with his perceptions about the French Foreign Legion."

Andreas's brow furrowed and a frown formed slowly on his face. I pressed on.

"But it's OK, because I realize that on this voyage, for the first time, I have made my peace with those men. I have forgiven them."

Andreas erupted, slapping his forehead. "You don't need to *forgive* your fathers! That's practically irrelevant!"

Then he softened a little. "They were just a bunch of guys trying to get through life, each dealing with their own troubles. You went to war to prove to yourself that you had value as a man—do you realize how twisted that is? No, there's more to this! There is something, *someone,* missing. Do you realize who this is?"

Recognition dawned, but before I could respond he spoke for me. "It's your mother. Your mother! All of the crap you are putting yourself through—honor, duty, responsibilities that you believe must be fulfilled at any cost—all of this baggage and guilt that you carry is because of the decisions your mother made when you were a child. She decided to leave your natural father. She decided to marry an abusive man. She decided to stay married to a man who regularly beat and abused her children. *She* is the person that you need to talk to. You need to speak to her and confront *her*. *She* made these decisions, and yet *you* have chosen to ignore the consequences and have made other people around you suffer. You should make your peace with *her* because her decisions have led you on a quest for happiness, which you are still seeking."

My mind raced, Roman candles of realization bursting through to awareness. But I felt honor bound to do defend her. "But she did her best. She didn't have qualifications or skills to make enough money and felt she needed a man to support her. This was back in the seventies. But she still loved us with all her heart. She is a good mother! She even left the abusive husband eventually. So she did do something about it because it became intolerable for her, too."

Andreas was slowly shaking his head side to side; I clearly didn't get it. He pulled his chair so close to mine that our knees were almost touching. His face loomed less than a foot away from mine. Slowly he raised a giant chubby finger and jabbed it gently into my chest, right into my heart. "Alex, my brother," he said, "you are good. You are a good man!'

He looked at me with tears in his eyes.

"You don't appreciate who or what you are! And you're no different from millions of others. Each person on Earth is special, a divine human being. Yet, like you, so many people have so little self-worth because of their beliefs and their choices. From this moment on you can always, always choose to be happy. Do you understand this yet?"

He sat back slowly. He had me exposed—wide, wide open. And while a part of me knew he must have fed these lines to countless other argonauts, still his delivery was devastating. I covered my face with my hands, embarrassed at the emotions my face betrayed.

"Listen," he whispered, with the utmost gentleness, "I know how you feel. Who hasn't been messed up by their parents in one form or another? I had a similar experience. My mother married a stepfather who beat me. And yet she chose to stay with him for thirty years! But

I don't let this affect me. I have made peace with my mother, and you need to make your peace with yours."

Even as the profundity of this counsel sunk in, I asked one final—and very unrelated—question. "Andreas, on this voyage some people were saying that you are running a cult."

He sighed, then frowned slightly. "The people that say these things . . ." He paused. "It comes from a place of fear. They have nothing to fear and neither do you. Please don't be scared about anything anymore. Always remember from now on that fear is a choice. A choice. Happiness is a choice and so is courage. You must have the courage to always choose happiness. It is important you know the real meaning of life—to be happy, to learn, and to love. Nothing is more important than these three things.'"

He put his hand on my shoulder and for the last time said, "Everything is as it should be."

He stood, ready to embrace me. As we parted I felt a huge burden lift. I actually physically felt lighter. I walked away to think. I gazed in semihypnosis at the river, contemplating that this mysterious man had given me insights that had the power to change my outlook forever. I thought of my son and felt a wave of longing. I simply couldn't wait to get back to him. He needed me and I needed him—we must be together for us both to thrive.

Time to go home.

Epilogue

I felt rejuvenated, believing I could return to civilization and start a new chapter with my family with an entirely different approach to life. The gift was optimism and compassion and understanding that the world is an organic entity; no life-form exists in spectacular isolation; almost all species cocreate a mutual dependency on their organic habitat and on others. I knew now we can glimpse mysterious detectable realms of life that exist in that ephemeral space we call the ether, masked from our precious but ordinary sensory perception. We must be bold and continue to explore them. Create and collaborate with them, then harness the power because creativity really is "evolution in our very own hands."

Back in Iquitos I said my good-byes to the argonauts, including Andreas. His parting words were typically enigmatic. "And remember . . . there is still a voyage inside of you."

As I said good-bye to Ben, he said, "There is always freedom in choice. This is the beauty of free will! You can choose to have responsibilities—or not. Either choice is in itself a beautiful thing. Choice *is* freedom. And integrity is not just about honor, trust, and responsibility; it's also about being true to your choices."

Part of me didn't want to leave this beautiful country, with its strange plant potion. Ayahuasca, Andreas, and Richard had provided opportunities to explore aspects of myself I might not have otherwise ever had the chance to. Ayahuasca showed me the highs and lows, the light and the dark. Andreas had challenged beliefs and judgments. Each day had been a quest into mystery.

During the flight home I reflected on the changes in my life over the past year and imagined having a conversation with my grandfather, a wing commander in the Air Force during the Second World War. Though I loved him with all my heart, as a strictly scotch and cigarettes guy, I felt sure he wouldn't understand my choices, especially about coming to the Amazon and seeking awareness. I imagined him saying, "Son, all these crazy thoughts you're having and these visions you see when you drink that ayahuasca stuff, it's superficial, all in your head. It's not real."

But that was not true. I had undergone a transformational shift, a reboot, something seismically disruptive, and I did not have the remotest concern whether it had occurred inside my head or outside, because the result—a fresh burst of creative thinking and a new respect for mankind and nature—was emotionally real enough. As to this hypothetical argument common to the straight world that says visions aren't real and consequently have no value—it was irrelevant to me. My assessment of ayahuasca's value, while heretical to much of the mainstream world, was relevant to *me*. My experiences, I felt sure, would forever affect my beliefs, actions, and feelings. We only get to experience one reality—our own. So, irrespective of the fact that everything I experienced could be a delusion, it was a healthy one for me—much like a placebo. My grandfather had been a brave man, but this whole topic of altered states of consciousness would, I am certain, have prompted within him a fear-based reaction because it was of the *unknown*. He had a traditional mind-set and believed what his leaders told him—his leaders always knew best. Maybe it was generational: he can keep his Frank Sinatra; I'll roll with the Beatles. All I knew was that having this imaginary conversation with him helped me clarify my feelings and even cement a few certainties.

The strangeness of the ayahuasca experience, combined with the sense of connection to a higher intelligence and power, was undeniable. I often wondered if it was possible to have one without the other—probably not. But, based on experience, it damn well made spiritual growth more colorful to me than anything Old World religion had to offer. It is important to me not to confuse peak moments with religion—that's what religious people do. Dangerously, they ascribe moments of bliss to a savior instead of to consciousness. The focus on a found truth—the inevitable "my savior is better than yours"—only creates division, when it is unity we need. Our brains are running a 100,000-year-old operating system that's no longer relevant in an imminently dawning age of abundance.

Even as I tried to maintain a balanced view, I returned home inspired and evangelized about the power of ayahuasca. I resigned from the military, settling back into civilian life. Everything felt good. I looked at the world differently, with a fresh optimistic perspective. My marriage was stronger because my wife had trusted me to return from this odyssey. She had found her own spiritual path long before me, and now, at last, I could identify with that aspect of her nature. Most important, I was calmer, convinced that my death will not be the end. Death is just another transformation, and in realizing this I have returned from war and the Amazon unhindered by unnecessary mortal burdens. I carry myself more lightly. My mother and I have talked about our relationship, moving on from the past and looking forward to the bright future we still share. We are fully at peace. We love each other.

The war and ayahuasca made me face many of my own fears. And I understand a lot more about what fear is. Many ancient wisdom texts have revealed that the opposite of love is not hate but fear. In Helmand, in the filth of war, the marine mentality is to use all of the physical senses all of the time to detect threats, which is the mentality of animals in the wild. Fear serves them, and us, at the basest level—that of survival. For all the good of the higher, more abstract values that the marines instill—honor, commitment, self-sacrifice—this basic survival instinct is foundational. The problem is that this survival instinct is foundational to us all, even when our survival is *not* threatened. We function too often from a fear-based self-interest, mostly in "me" mode (what's in it for me?), rather than "we" mode. My experiences in the Amazon led me to an understanding that consciousness and intelligence cannot evolve rapidly and healthily when we are predominantly in the me state of mind. By moving from fear to trust, peace, and, ultimately, love, we enrich not only our own lives but the greater good.

Andreas and Richard, and other pioneers like them at the extreme frontiers, are contributing to the evolution of global consciousness. Andreas and ayahuasca were a particularly potent combination. He is an enigma and unmatched polymath, a renaissance man, larger than several lives. I am particularly indebted to him because my fear-based frame of reference led me to doubt him, and I now realize he is a brave man who has surmounted enormous personal challenges. We should not check our healthy skepticism or good sense at the door of expanded perception, but at the very least we do have to be willing to probe into our own biases to see where we are fooling or blinding ourselves. Like Andreas, the truth-teller is sometimes disguised as a trickster, the prophet as a fool. Sometimes the only way to crack the wall of our resistance is to put ourselves in situations that are not only unfamiliar but downright uncomfortable. The Mythic Voyage was bizarre—but good bizarre, beautiful bizarre.

Needless to say, the ayahuasca ceremonies in the Amazon were some of the most profound experiences of my life. Ayahuasca taught me many things, and one of the most important is that we always have choice. We have the power to choose our beliefs and our attitudes. And a more empathetic civilization makes sense. The more separate we become, the more conflicts will arise. When you realize that profound joy, peace, and love reside innately in all of us—when this realization is not instilled as a belief but *experienced* as true—you cannot easily forget this or indeed would ever want to. You cannot unlearn such a teaching.

For all their benefits, entheogens and ayahuasca are not for everyone. Many people don't want to relinquish control of themselves, even for a few minutes. That's understandable. It can be alarming, especially the first few times. But over time, you begin to develop a trust in the glory of this sacred plant. The indigenous peoples say that ayahuasca is a being—they call her Mother Ayahuasca. Like most mothers, she both loves and admonishes. It is said that she shows you what you are ready to see. And just about everyone who has been under her tutelage agrees that what they see is beyond description and sometimes beyond belief. That is precisely the point.

Yet, surrender cannot be partial. To find out who you *truly* are, you have to let go of everything you *think* you are going to discover. As boundaries dissolve—even temporarily—you get a glimpse of the whole, of which we are each a precious part. The word *entheogen* means engendering the divine within, finding the God within. Isn't *that* worth surrendering your fear to experience for a few hours? You don't need to keep repeating the experience once you get that you are God and God is you. That's why I rarely use entheogens anymore. But there is always more to learn, to explore.

Life is an adventure. To truly live life and deprogram, we have to become adventurers. After the war I sensed an opportunity to free myself from shackles snapped shut from earliest childhood: from my upbringing, education, religion, institutions, media, and authority figures. Breaking free is an ongoing process. But the victory, really, is to realize that you are shackled in the first place and to dare yourself to set yourself free. And so—I dare you. Because one thing I've learned for sure is this: everybody dies, but not everybody lives.

Using the Shamanic Experience for Healing Trauma

Veterans are the light at the tip of the candle,
illuminating the way for the whole nation. If veterans can
achieve awareness, transformation, understanding and
peace, they can share with the rest of society the realities
of war. And they can teach us how to make peace with
ourselves and each other, so we never have to use violence
to resolve conflicts again.

THICH NHAT HANH, ZEN MASTER BUDDHIST MONK

An Idea Begins to Form

On the final day, as we sailed back to Iquitos, I knew it would take me a long time to assimilate the experiences from the Mythic Voyage. An idea began to form. If I could be inspired by the Amazon, then other veterans could be. The contrast between Afghanistan and the Amazon was staggering. Serenity, harmony—this Eden had it all, and I knew now that it had the potential to inspire men out of maudlin, postwar introspection and despair and perhaps offer a climax to each person's odyssey, a landmark initiation and regenerative rite of passage. I mused about what might be.

Currently, no ceremonial restoration process exists for veterans to acknowledge the duality of the good and evil we experience as humans. Men have to muddle through in their own way, and many never achieve integration. They experience too much bitterness and anger as they try to fit back into society, while still dragging behind them the weight of the chaos they were just immersed in. The experience of pain makes the preciousness of true peace all the more exquisite. Choosing war, even for noble reasons, can be a doubled-edged sword, and this is why, following service, choosing its opposite—immersion in natural bliss—can be so valuable.

Many pacifists seem incapable of grasping the fact that some people are born defenders; it is primal. They are driven to serve in what they believe at the time to be justifiable conflicts—protect the weak and fight injustice. And so, for *that* person, his or her opportunity to experience both these polarities—war (for the right reasons) followed by bliss—can enable him or her to grow and develop, perhaps restoring personal peace.

In the years since the Afghan war started, so many men had encountered extreme conflict and stress that I began to get a hunch that the way to deal with it was not to bury the experiences, masking them with pharmaceuticals or alcohol, but to *confront* them in a safe setting in a majestic environment. We could create ceremonies and rituals that are currently missing from a veteran's decompression process. We should bring ayahuasca legally to the northern hemisphere and create rituals that honor the choices that these men and women have made—regardless of whether history ultimately judges a war to have been won or lost, morally right or wrong. After all, when someone makes the choice to go to war, he or she is operating with only limited information. The tricky part is making choices that you think are good, knowing that history may ultimately deem them bad. Only time will tell if you chose the right side to fight on.

Meanwhile, society needs to act now, while the veteran still lives and is still seeking healing and, ultimately, understanding. Working with an experienced shaman in a ceremony could help acknowledge that goodness and wonder exist in a complicated world where evil seems to widely prevail. Ayahuasca might be the "good medicine" and opportunity for regenesis that so many veterans need, to help them integrate paradoxes and acknowledge that the choice to serve was altruistic. Such ceremonies might reinforce the notion that collectively, as a species, we are good—that the veterans are still good, despite what may have happened to them and those around them in the war. Each of us could move forward, and together we could make better choices; at the very least we would learn. Veterans will become more than they were, more readily capable of teaching. Motivated veterans will pass on the knowledge of how to be good and how to inspire others. This was my emerging hope. And some of it was borne out over the coming years, as more and more veterans began heading to the Amazon for the healing potential of ayahuasca.

The Next Step

By writing this book my sincere intention is to heighten the awareness of interested veterans to the potential healing experience of South American shamanism. Alternate states of consciousness and military culture traditionally had mixed like oil and water—until now. The building of the bridge between the military and psychedelics is underway. There are already medical doctors in the Amazon advocating integrative approaches to medicine as well as Vietnam veterans self-medicating with ayahuasca, forging themselves a new path to redemption where convention and pharmaceuticals failed them. We will need to encourage the judicious application of disruptive thinking to break down the remaining barriers.

Shamanism can take place without the ingestion of a psychedelic or an entheogen. For those of a bolder nature (and there are no shortage of these people in the services), integrative treatments could be extended to incorporate the use of ayahuasca. Extensive scientific research is already under way to treat veterans with PTSD with the psychoactive drug MDMA. Ayahuasca is 100 percent natural and could be used in conjunction with MDMA or as an alternative. There is still much work to be done, and we will need to tread carefully. It's not for the meek, but neither was Afghanistan. Every man or woman there had been a willing volunteer to go and fight. The Amazon experience is safer and infinitely more inspirational. Yes, it might blow your mind for a few hours taking you "out of this world," but the elixir also has the capacity to leave sunshine in your heart. I figure that, given the opportunity, many veterans will welcome the chance to go.

The conventional approach to dealing with PTSD is with pharmaceutical drugs—which is a Band-Aid approach to solving the real problem. Veterans have earned the right to choose how they heal. A retreat to the Amazon offers the potential to deliver what many ex-servicemen still want—adventure and a challenge. They *want* to be tested. Ayahuasca will test you. This approach to healing is not for the faint of heart. Of course, there is always the option to offer a mild or a wild experience, depending on the needs of each man or woman. Many veterans still have a cavalier and buccaneering spirit that attracts them to risk. Working with ayahuasca has the potential to grant them that, plus the added potential for a metaphysical experience, a direct sense of connection to the Creator, to the divine, to diminish anxiety and fear of death.

Experiencing alternative states of consciousness brought about by consuming psychoactive plants is not illegal in most South American countries. Indigenous peoples and even some governments respect that nature has given us this resource. Clearly, ayahuasca is not a potential healing solution applicable to everyone, but if it helps even a few veterans assimilate back into the society, then it has its place. All it asks of you is the will and a good intention.

Of course, it's not just veterans who can benefit from exploring their consciousness. Millions of people experience trauma and suffering. The choice to stick with conventional medicine will always remain for those that want it, but there are alternatives, such as natural plant substances that alter consciousness and can raise self-awareness. When you take entheogens in the right setting and in the right dose, you don't need faith to help you connect to the metaphysical. But what you do need is courage to take the step—not much, just enough to provide you with new direct personal *experiences*. In turn, these experiences will provide you with the foundation upon which to construct new, more fulfilling, life-sustaining beliefs.

Some Practical Advice

Nearly everything we do in life is either to minimize pain or maximize pleasure, and psychedelics can take you to heaven or to hell. For every uplifting and inspiring story you hear, there are always the bad stories—people becoming frightened, losing control, or feeling paranoid. Bad trips can be averted, and if they aren't averted, then they can be managed. There are plenty of inner explorers who have charted the territory for us, so it behooves anyone thinking of using entheogens to learn the "rules."

Start by doing your research. Talk to people who have had the experience. Read books on the subject. Join related forums on the Internet and leverage first-class websites. Here are a few recommendations to get you started:

Erowid.org. An excellent nonprofit educational organization that provides information about psychoactive plants and chemicals that can produce altered states of consciousness.

Vetentheogenic.org. VET (Veterans for Entheogenic Therapy) is a 501.C3 nonprofit organization—"healing veterans one plant at a time." Founded by United States Marine Corps Infantry veteran Ryan LeCompte to help spread awareness about alternative medicines for the treatment of PTSD in veterans. They have one mission: heal fellow vets through plant medicine and mindfulness-based therapeutic practices.

Maps.org. MAPS (Multidisciplinary Association for Psychedelic Studies) is a foremost nonprofit research and education organization that applies professional scientific rigor to psychedelic research therapy and education.

Reset.me. An amazing online resource created by former CNN news reporter Amber Lyon who suffered from work-related PTSD and then healed herself.

Set and setting are vital. Get the dosage right. Measure it precisely. Start cautiously. Finally, it is wise to prepare to integrate the experience into your life, something you do to get to know yourself more deeply, and so it can take months to integrate. Don't rush into the next experience before you have explored the insights from the last one. Sometimes that means weeks, months, or even years.

If you follow these rules, you will reduce the chances for having a dark or frightening episode. As the shamans say, the plant teachers take you where you need to go, and sometimes you have to descend into the dark before you are ready to emerge into the light. If you do have a rough experience, there are ways to manage it. One technique is to sing. Everything is a vibration, and the internal vibrations made from singing can help shift the energy of your consciousness. Sacred song—or vibration—is integral to the ceremonies conducted by most Amazonian shamans and by many other kinds of shamans in different contexts. In ayahuasca ceremonies, these sacred or magical songs are called icaros. Using only a few lines of an icaro, an ayahuasquero can shift your consciousness as if it were attached to a string, moving you from one state to another with a melodic tug here and another one there. When your mind seems to be descending into the dark and you don't want to go there, or stay there, take the initiative. It's *your* mind after all—change it! And remember that this too shall pass. Sometimes you really can just wait it out.

Perhaps the biggest challenge to a bad trip—and to breaking through to a sublime one—is giving up control of the ego. The ego is easily threatened when it feels it is not in control, and it will resist surrendering for all it's worth. Letting go can be a real challenge, as it feels as if you are losing your identity, maybe even dying. If you can remember what the struggle really is about—loosening the grip of your ego and not your actual death—you can move past the struggle and release yourself fully into the visions and insights.

These widely acknowledged rules can help you reap precious rewards. You may experience ecstasy as you never have before. You may feel the boundaries of yourself dissolving as you realize your rightful place within the web of life, existing in a state of graced unity, at one with the divine.

To the shamans, there are untold numbers of dimensions and beings. Shamans make it a life study to explore these realms and figure out the way they work. For example, it is common for people using psychedelics such as psilocybin, mescaline, and ayahuasca to see—and even engage with—entities that appear to be entirely alien. Such contact can be mind blowing. There is a well-known story of an anthropologist who, during an ayahuasca journey, encountered batlike aliens claiming that they were going to take over the world. They and their threats were very frightening. When he recounted this experience to the shaman the next day, the shaman remarked casually, "Oh, don't worry. They're always doing that."

The shamans have already encountered anything you will, and so they know how to respond. Their knowledge can greatly assist. They rarely assign moral judgment to a bizarre or frightening scenario. They are pragmatic and have navigated these strange otherworldly realms professionally. They are not easily tricked by the spirits, beings, and whatever else from other dimensions. That's why in some South American languages, the word for shaman literally means "clever fella."

Psychedelics, intelligently combined with science, are the "on-ramp" for the truly magical road to enlightenment. They are the power *and* force. Thanks to the Internet, the genie is out of the bottle. It is now clear that humankind is vibrating at a much higher frequency and shining with more brightness and intensity than most people realize. The whole of humanity is entitled to these free and abundant plant teachers, which, coupled with the right intentions, steer us to what some may call our *Homo luminous* destiny.